Why Churches Die

BY
HOLLIS L.
GREEN

A Guide to Basic
Evangelism and
Church Growth

Bethany Fellowship
Minneapolis, Minn. **55438**

DEDICATION

This book is dedicated to my two sons, Barton and Brian, whose affection and respect for a "project oriented" dad has been a source of encouragement through the years.

Foreword

Many denominations in North America have ceased
growing. Some are declining. And this at a time when
less than half the citizens and the youth are practicing
Christians. Though the population is expanding, thousands of congregations are smaller now than they were
a few years ago.

Even worse, during the past war decades church
growth has often been regarded as materialistic, base,
and even disreputable. Derogating growth, evangelism,
and the very church itself is fashionable in some quarters.
Those who rightly stress that Christians should love mercy
and do justice, often erringly assert—or imply—that only
ethical action is true and relevant Christianity. While
churches sicken and die, while two billion have not yet
heard effectively the name of Jesus Christ, whole denominations spend almost all their resources on things
other than discipling men and women.

By way of contrast with all this, Dr. Hollis L. Green
recognizes the growth crisis and addresses this book
directly to it. He knows the American church well. He
speaks to real conditions. Wasting no time on superficial

considerations and easy diagnosis, he identifies thirty-five reasons "Why Churches Die" *and proposes remedial action for each.* His proposals are biblical and will be welcomed by dedicated Christians of every denomination. He calls for "total surrender to Christ," and "quality Christians." He insists as all church growth men do—that growth in grace must accompany growth in numbers.

This creative and optimistic book should be widely read by lay leaders and ministers. It is part of the wave of tomorrow. Church growth is obviously the will of God. We face highly winnable populations. The field has not ripened by accident. God has ripened it. God wants it reaped. Christians must dis-associate themselves from anti-harvest people who would snatch defeat out of the jaws of victory. This is the day to purify and magnify the church and multiply congregations of the redeemed. This is a day to liberate millions into the glorious liberty of Christ.

Justice will not prevail, righteousness will not flow as a mighty stream till we have multitudes of practicing Christians. This is the day of the common man. He has the vote now in almost every land. And too many common men are not disciples of Christ! The dangerous situation must not continue. Dr. Green's book shows us many ways to remedy it. He has made a notable contribution to the church in our day. His rich experience and wide acquaintance with modern congregations insures the relevance of his writing. Churches would help themselves if they would send copies to all their board or session members.

September 1, 1972

Donald A. McGavran
School of Missions and Institute
of Church Growth
Fuller Theological Seminary
Pasadena, California

Preface

This story about the old farmer and his excellent crop of corn points to a serious church growth problem. It seems that a city fellow was commenting on the excellent crop and telling the farmer how grateful he should be to God for the sunshine, the rain and the minerals in the ground. After listening to the lengthy exhortation on gratitude to God for His work in causing the corn to grow, the farmer retaliated: "You should have seen the field when God had it by Himself!" This story clearly points to the necessity for human involvement in God's work through the church. As the uncultivated field, there can be no production without man's participation in the divine plan. It is my firm belief that when man cooperates with the laws of God and nature, the church will grow.

Since the human element is a basic problem with church growth, this book concerns itself with human involvement in the divine plan. No one will deny that God is working in the world today. The basic problem of the church is cooperation with the divine plan. Since God is working, it is a matter of men getting together and participating in the work of God.

The distinctiveness of Luke's theology has become increasingly apparent to me in recent years. Being a well-educated Greek and a traveled physician, Luke did not merely transmit the tradition as it came to him. He was both a theologian and a historian interpreting the Christian message from a vantage point of understanding and experience. As an interpreter, Luke writes out of a unique theological background strongly influenced by his relationship with the Apostle Paul. He gives the most complete account of the life of Jesus that has survived. His gospel covers "all that Christ began to do and teach" from His birth to the ascension. In his second book, the Acts, he carries the history of the Christian Church forward until the Christian message is established in Rome, the ultimate goal in Paul's ministry.

Luke's theology cannot be understood until his concern for the human element is discovered and understood as a frame of reference for his writings. Luke's style and the particular way in which he puts his text together points to this objective. All scripture is given by inspiration of God but we are aware that the writer was given certain liberties to arrange materials and that the Holy Spirit used the language and experience of the writer for natural expression.

Luke's writings show him to be preoccupied with the human element and how man fits into God's plan. This is shown primarily in his selection of parables and the incidences he chooses to relate in the life and teaching of Jesus. He seemed to deliberately adapt his message to this objective.

In this respect I am partial to the writings of Dr. Luke. His two books comprise over one-fourth of the New Testament. This very fact points to the importance of his contribution to the preservation of the New Testament way of life. His gospel has been called "the most beautiful book ever written." He was the friend of the underdog, the Gentiles, the Samaritans, women and children. He tells us of the good Samaritan, the Prodigal, the unjust steward and the rich fool. Luke was a man of prayer; he gave more attention to prayer than any other gospel writer, yet he presents Jesus Christ as the Son of Man and emphasizes the human element in the divine plan. He traveled extensively with the Apostle Paul throughout the Gentile world and seems to understand the working of the New Testament Church. He actually lived in the post-apostolic age. This means that his situation and the circumstances of his ministry were akin to ours.

It is my belief that Luke, being a medical doctor and a church historian, trained to analyze and diagnose the real causes and implications of certain symptoms, looked at the New Testament Church more objectively than most New Testament personalities. He analyzed not the surface symptoms, but looked for the real problem. Space would not permit an analysis of Luke's two books, but his objective, his concern for the human involvement in the divine plan has been the motivating principle behind the writing of this book.

The book is an outgrowth of twenty years of personal ministry and active study in the field of church growth and basic evangelism. Both primary and general research were conducted on the subject in South America, the Far East, the United Kingdom, Europe and the United States. Most church growth material concerns world missions, i.e. church growth in Asia, Africa and Latin America. I have carefully studied materials written by teachers and career missionaries who have studied at the Institute of Church Growth in Pasadena. I am convinced that the principles and procedures laid down by Donald McGavran, for example, in his *Understanding Church Growth* (Eerdmans, 1970), for overseas missions are applicable in North America. The principles must of course be adapted. Very little application of these "foreign" works have been made to the church at home. I have used these sources in developing this application and gratefully acknowledge my indebtedness to them. Applying them to the American church has been my privilege.

The principles of growth and progress are universal. The forces which are at work in missions fields are also working in the USA. During the past four years, I have traveled across the USA conducting Saturday Seminars, clergy and lay retreats, workshops and personal interviews on the general subject. From these sessions, from personal research and readings, from knowledge gathered here and there, I have determined thirty-five basic reasons I believe the church is not growing. Under the title WHY CHURCHES DIE these reasons are classified in five categories: program centered problems; personnel centered problems; organization centered problems; fellowship centered problems; renewal centered problems.

Hollis L. Green, Th.D.

Contents

Money, Meatloaf and Mimeograph

(Program-Centered Problems)

Many problems of the church are program centered. Basically, Christianity has lost its Sunday punch because the first day of the week has become the psychological last day. Consequently, it no longer sets the pace and pattern for the activities of the week. This precipitates a theology of coercion that causes the clergy to spend most of their time attempting to challenge and motivate constituency involvement in the Great Commission. This theology of coercion breeds a methodology designed to reach men and almost negates the power of personal Christian experience. Complicated methods and overprogramming limits the mobilization of the congregation because the constituency does not understand. When program fails, often the people are blamed. Thus, the church becomes imprisoned by previous patterns and perpetuates programs that are ineffective. Perhaps the greatest problem of all is that the church building complex which should be the force with which to work, becomes the field of operation. Consequently, in the hustle to keep the organization alive, clergy and congregants are often unaware that the organism is dying.

1. Christianity Has Lost Its Sunday Punch
2. Great Commission Is Misunderstood
3. Methods Are Considered a Means to Reach Men
4. Programming Limits Mobilization
5. Church Is Imprisoned by Previous Patterns
6. Base Becomes the Field of Operations
7. Congregation Is Unaware of Dying Organism

1.

Christianity Has Lost Its Sunday Punch

Many churches are impotent and powerless to grow numerically. Some are failing to grow spiritually and at times seem not to be growing at all. Why do some churches fight a losing battle? Does the gospel have no power to transform lives and to transfer the interests of men from themselves to Jesus Christ? Is God different from what He was in the days of the Apostles? Was God more concerned about the early believers than He is in Christians of today? What has happened to Christianity's "Sunday punch" that turned the world upside down in Apostolic days?

An easygoing leisurely approach to Sunday causes Christians to be indifferent about their worship and witness all week. Consequently, they have no daily devotional life and little or no personal witness. Accepting Monday as the psychological beginning of the week makes one materialistic and preoccupied with the problems of life. God gave man a day of rest. He has stretched it out to two and is going for three.

If a man should live his full "three score and ten" years, he would live ten years of Sundays. It is safe to predict that the value of any man's life will be determined by what he does on those ten years of Sundays. Sunday is not a day of rest neither is it the last day of the week as the "hurry, worry, work-a-day" culture seems to suggest and which many Christians practice. Sunday is the first day and sets the pace and pattern for the week.

Sunday, the first day of the week, has always been important to God. It was on the first day that God did His major work of re-creation—of bringing order out of chaos. God created light and initiated His works of division on the first day. He separated light from darkness and established the eternal principle of separation on the basis of difference.

Contrary to popular belief the first day of the week was important in the spiritual history of Israel (Leviticus 23). The "morrow after the sabbath" was used by God to typically suggest significant spiritual truths that have been revealed in the New Testament. It was following Israel's first annual gathering for the Passover that the pattern began. The Feast of Unleavened Bread started on the first day after the Sabbath Passover and represented purity of heart and life following redemption. This week-long feast speaks of communion with Christ and the full blessings of His redemption. It suggests a consistent holy walk Sunday through Sunday.

Is it not also significant that the wave offering during the Feast of the Firstfruits was waved on the "morrow after the Sabbath"? This first day feast speaks clearly of Christ's resurrection and spiritual hope in Him (I Corinthians 15:20-23). The Feast of Pentecost was on the "morrow after the Sabbath" and was characterized by wave-loaves representing the spiritual union of believers in one homogeneous body. Sacrifice, worship, and spiritual activity characterized these "first day" gatherings of God's people. The "morrow after the Sabbath" meetings were called holy convocations or an assembly of persons called together by summons. They were to do no "servile" work, which is to say, no servant or slave labor that suggests work for an employer; this does not exclude labor for the Lord and His cause.

Sunday was important to early Christianity. The first day of the week became the Christian day of worship in remembrance of Christ's resurrection. The fact that Paul uses "the first day of the week" in I Corinthians 16:2 seems to suggest that "the Lord's day" was not a widely used expression until later. The scriptural authority for the expression is not found until John's writing (Revelation 1:10). First day worship became the custom early in the life of the church although it was not the only day on which services were held. Most likely because of the "slave culture" the earliest services began on Saturday evening at the close of the Jewish Sabbath and continued throughout the night, climaxing in an observance of the Lord's Supper (Acts 20:7, 11).

Sunday worship is definitely associated with Christ's resurrection. Christ sanctified the first day of the week by His resurrection and emphasized it by making another appearance to the disciples on Sunday (John 20:26). The Holy Spirit was also sent to the waiting believers on the first day of the week (Acts 2). This seems to be a clear fulfillment of a pattern suggested in the feasts of Israel. It seems that the early believers began their week with worship and active witness and this pattern and pace was maintained throughout the week:

> And they, continuing daily with one accord in the temple, and breaking bread from house to house, did eat their meat with gladness and singleness of heart, praising God, and having favor with all the people. And the Lord added to the church daily such as should be saved (Acts 2:46, 47).

The first day gatherings of the early church included reading the writings of the apostles and prophets, exhortation, prayer, and the Lord's Supper, and the collection (Justin: A.D. 150; Apol i. 65). The Apostolic

Church failed to name a particular day of rest among the necessary things of Acts 15:28, 29; and clearly taught that even though worship was held on a particular day (Sunday) it did not sanctify the day any more than any other (Romans 14:5, 6). Although daily gatherings initially characterized the early church, Sunday, the first day, gradually became the distinctive day for worship (Acts 20:7; I Corinthians 16:2). The Lord's Day is nowhere present in the New Testament as a fulfillment of the Sabbath even though other features of Christianity are presented in comparison with Jewish ordinances (I Corinthians 10:16-21; Colossians 2:11; Hebrews 10:22). This silence is especially marked in Hebrews, where the Sabbath is only mentioned as a type of the believer's rest (Hebrews 4).

Sunday is important to the Christian and the church today. In addition to the acceptance of the first day convocations, the New Testament seems to reverse the old order. The Old Testament order was first work and then a sabbath for rest; but this order was reversed by the resurrection of Christ. Abraham Kuyper in *The Work of the Holy Spirit* aptly expressed this reversal: "In the beginning, the week closed with the Sabbath; for us the day of the resurrection of Christ opens the week which feeds upon the powers of that resurrection."

From the beginning, God's ultimate pattern for redeemed men seems clear. The first day of the week was to be for worshiping and witnessing. Five days were allotted for man to work for his family and to acquire the means to materially support the work of the kingdom, and the seventh day was set aside to rest, reminisce and recuperate from all his labors.

Modern man's transformation of Sunday into a day of leisure and pleasure has taken the "Sunday punch" out of the work of the church! Sunday should be a day of worship and active witness to set the pace and pattern for the coming week; not the last day of the work week—an afterthought or suffix to living. Sunday was designed to usher God's people into a week of active partnership and participation in the work of the kingdom.

It was a "Sunday punch" that catapulted the New Testament Church into the homes and daily lives of believers. They sought first the kingdom of God on the first day of the week. This set the pace and pattern for life and living throughout the remaining days. The careless, indifferent and commercial approach to Sunday has robbed the day of its first day qualities and caused it to become the psychological last day of the week. This is one of the basic causes for Christianity losing the impact on the world which characterized the New Testament Church.

Early Christianity's "Sunday punch" gave a new, fresh, and positive outlook on life and caused Christians to place material gain and personal pleasure in the positive context of the church and the Christian life. When Christians sacrifice their Sunday afternoon nap or pleasure ride and follow God's basic pattern of worship and witness, Christianity will recover the effectiveness that turned the world upside down in New Testament days. This will bring an advance of the Christian ministries of spiritual development, growth, and outreach and cause the church to be an adequate instrument in the hand of God to change the world.

A failure to adequately use the renewal aspects of the first day of the week brings about serious consequences for the church today. Among these difficulties is the development of a theology of coercion based on a misunderstanding of the Great Commission.

2.

Great Commission Is Misunderstood

The classic misunderstanding of the Great Commission has made it self-defeating by producing a theology of coercion in an effort to compel people to "go." Consequently, the clergy spends most of their time attempting to challenge and motivate involvement on the part of the congregation. No one seems to get excited about a command to go to everyone with everything. The selfishness of the human heart causes man to be concerned primarily about his own and it is difficult to express enthusiasm about some faraway place with a strange sounding name. It is easy to overlook someone down the block whose color or culture is different. Actually, the Commission must be experienced to be understood. It is not an order to "go," it is a plan of action for individuals who are in the process of "going." The "good news" of the gospel impels those who receive it to share their experience with others.

All true believers in Christ should participate in the life of the church because the abilities of each one are needed by all members. This love and concern, this bearing of one another's burdens, is a vital part of the ministry shared by laymen and clergymen alike. This recalls the "priesthood" of all believers and cannot be ignored without great peril and loss of essential quality in church growth. However, true involvement can come only from internal motivation. The "go ye" must be in the heart as well as in the head.

The church has two major emphases: evangelism and education. This is significantly brought out in the Commission. The resurrection completed the work of redemption and Pentecost thrust a band of Spirit-anointed witnesses into the world for service. The next thing on God's calendar is the consumating of the age. Meanwhile, what is the interim responsibility of the church?

It is the responsibility of Christians through the agency of the Holy Spirit to reach and teach all nations concerning the saving grace of Christ during the interim period. Out of the nature of His very being Christ commissioned the church to "make disciples." Christ never questioned the fact that His true followers would go; therefore, the "go ye" of the Great Commission (Matthew 28:10) is not necessarily an imperative, but an internal motivation to spiritual activity.[1] It is true that Jesus spoke Aramaic and that Aramaic and Hebrew participles were sometimes used as imperatives, but consensus places the emphasis of the Commission on the words "disciple all nations." Such confidence! As a participle "go" could be literally translated "going" or "as you go." Christ knew they would respond to His call; therefore, He gave them a program. As you go into all the world "teach" (make disciples) of all nations. The Commission was for followers already in motion. The "go ye" was placed automatically in the heart of New Testament converts. Conversion became their motivation.

Christ did not leave His work to chance. He spelled out the details. He did not even imply that His people would not go; hence the command, "As you go, disciple all nations." They were to go purposefully and teach men of Christ and lead them to an open declaration of allegiance to Him. Then once they came to a saving knowledge of Christ and were publicly initiated and identified with His cause on earth, they were to be trained and equipped for service in the church.

Since Christ has "all authority" in heaven and earth and commissioned His followers to "make disciples" as they traveled into all the world, the major item on God's agenda seems to be that of "making disciples." The explosion of the gospel caused people of the New Testament to take rapid growth for granted. They used net fishing and did not shrink from an influx of numbers regardless of culture or ethnic background. They were pulsatingly aware that all men needed the gospel of redemption and that Christ was the answer to man's dilemma. Everyone was welcomed into the family of God and felt at home in the fellowship of Christians.

A dramatic version of the Commission is the parable of the great feast which Luke accounts in Chapter 14. Everyone on the initial invitation list utterly rejected the call to the supper. The servant then anticipated and misunderstood his Lord's command and went beyond the selected list to seek out personally, groups of people who were obviously classified as blind, lame, etc., that the Lord's house might be filled.

The servant replied with some degree of pride that he had already done all the things that had been commanded yet the house was not filled. He had only invited them; the command was to "bring them in." This speaks so clearly of the smugness frequently encountered by churchmen and lay leaders who are busy with their little system of advancing the church, and say "we have tried this; it just doesn't work."

The Lord's insistent command was simple. "Go out into the highways and hedges and influence men to yield their lives and come in that my house may be filled [with worshipers]." The work was not easy, but they were to follow the plan laid down by the Master—that of making men into followers of Christ so that the Lord's House would be filled with worshipers.

Philips version of Ephesians 3:8-11 makes clear Paul's

expression of the inner workings of Christian motivation: "Yes, to me, less than the least of all Christians, has God given this grace, to enable me to proclaim to the Gentiles the incalculable riches of Christ, and to make plain to all men the meaning of that divine secret which He who created everything has kept hidden from the creation until now. The purpose is that all the angelic powers should now see the complex wisdom of God's plan being worked out through the church, in conformity to that timeless purpose which He centered in Christ our Lord." Not only was this the purpose of Paul's conversion and the mission of the Ephesian church, it is the purpose of all churches.

The basic outreach technique of the New Testament was personal witness. Personalized programs and basic spiritual renewal provide opportunities to eliminate a tragic weakness in many churches—the number of dumb disciples. Christians should witness. Wesley encouraged his people to "gossip the gospel." Gossip has present connotations that are unfortunate. Originally a gossiper was "a person spiritually related to another through being a sponosr at a baptism." The word literally means God-related. Therefore, when Wesley asked the people to "gossip the gospel" he intended that Christians be related to God and spiritually related to their friends by bringing them into a personal relationship with Jesus Christ.

The whole story of God's dealing with man is a record of His working with the individual in the context of community. Biblical scholars point out that a person comes to Christ, in part, as a member of a group or through the efforts of a group (Romans 10:8-17). God does not detach Himself from the world of men. He seeks them and confronts them with God-related men. A creative and spiritual interaction of men, striving together to hear exactly what God says to them, becomes a medium by which God continues to confront, control, and challenge the church.

The ultimate revelation of God is that of a person speaking to persons. God incarnate in Jesus Christ, the

"Word made flesh," spake and continues to speak to men through Spirit-filled believers. When a person meets Christ somehow all that he is and does speaks to other men of Jesus Christ. Conversion then changes the whole person—every area of life. The Holy Spirit then takes these men and creates an atmosphere of "togetherness" in which the truth can be communicated. Men should not feel pride at success in Christian service; it is the Holy Spirit who creates real fellowship (*koinonia*) and draws men to Christ and to one another. Here the language of relationship as well as the language of words, work together to determine the nature of communication.

The church must be careful not to overaccentuate motivation based on human needs. The offering of incentive and rewards often motivates men to become very much involved in activity and not sufficiently involved in spiritual living. Fear motivation can be used to the discredit of the church and the gospel as well.

Provided the New Testament is rightly divided, it is clearly evident that it concerns Christ, the Christian, and the two together—Christianity (Mark 16:19, 20). The Word tells of Christ on the throne, the task of the Christian and the ultimate triumph of Christianity. Note the sequence of the New Testament account: Christ commissioned His disciples, ascended to heaven; sat down on the right hand of God; the disciples went forth, and preached everywhere; the Lord confirmed His Word. Christ on the throne in heaven; Christians to the task on earth. The Savior in the place of authority; the servants in the place of testimony. Jesus enthroned—and the disciples with power from above set out to evangelize the hostile world—and in the language of their enemies, they began "to turn the world upside down."

The church appears in the New Testament as Christ's living body of called out ones. It existed, not out of the world shielded by four walls and stained-glass windows, but in the world as a witnessing community, sharing in love with every man the message of Christ. This must be the continuing challenge to the church—Christians are men with a mission, " . . . sent out ones . . . " called to enthusiastically witness through love. There is no end to the growth of a church that steps out in faith, armed with spiritual concepts and concentrating on a central idea—that of going everywhere preaching the gospel expecting God to confirm His Word.

It is true that the church is a separate group of blood-washed believers but this separation is not to be isolation. In addition to fellowship, believers are separated from the world that they may be equipped and trained for Christian service and witness. Jesus requested that the Father not take His disciples out of the world but "keep them from the evil." Christ wanted His followers in the world to finish the work of carrying the gospel to all nations. True believers will go back into the world as Christian witnesses and will by life and lip testify to the saving grace of Jesus Christ.

In the early days of the Salvation Army, William Booth was criticized for his noisy street meetings. He replied: "When I hear your church bells ringing they seem to be saying, 'Come to church! Come to church!' but the people do not come." The Army's big drum seems to say: "Fetch'em! Fetch'em! and that's what we do—and we get 'em." This points to the subtle reversal of the Commission in many places. The Commission no longer says "as you go" to the saint, it seems to address the sinner and says "you must come." This is tragic for the growth of the church.

3.

Methods
Are Considered a
Means to Reach Men

A theology of coercion breeds an artificial motivation that negates the power of personal experience which is the true means of advancing Christianity. In fact, personal experience is the key to New Testament power. A true conversion experience together with the Commission of Christ can become the true motivation to Christian action. This is the means that can move men forward in faith and thrust them into the world as witnesses.

A primary task of leadership is creating a church climate conducive to spiritual experience and growth.[2] Three things are prerequisite to a New Testament atmosphere in which growth can take place. New Testament means must be used to produce New Testament men who feel at home with New Testament methods. Means, men and methods should be in that *order*. A reverse order is often attempted, when methods are used in an effort to produce men in order to have the means to build the church. This approach is weak if not entirely backwards.

New Testament means is the power of the gospel: the power of spiritual experience in the lives of individuals. Paul says: "For our gospel came not unto you in word only, but also in power and in the Holy Ghost and in much assurance as you know what manner of men we were among you for your sakes" (I Thessalonians 1: 5). He talks about "our gospel," the good news of what happened to us.

Paul declared that testimony, witnessing, preaching, proclamation, gospelizing, telling the "good news" did not come just in vocabulary (human speech), but also in power. He seems to suggest that the power is inherent in the word of a testimony. The power is not in the human speech of the convert, but in the word of the testimony. When the word of the testimony is valid and victorious, it has life-giving force. The "good news" came not only in the Word, but in power and in Spirit. Actually, the testimony of "good news," the power of the personal experience, was delivered under the inspiration and the enthusiasm of the Holy Spirit. After all, "God in you" is the meaning of enthusiasm. Paul's witness came in much assurance, actually it was "crammed full of conviction." Speaking for Silas and Timothy he said: our testimony, our gospel, our words came not in human vocabulary alone but with power in the testimony of itself; and the Holy Spirit anointed the witness. They were convinced that the power that transformed them could do the same for all who hear. This power of personal experience transformed the New Testament world.

When Paul used the word "gospel," he was not thinking about the story facts in Matthew, Mark, Luke and John. These facts were probably not yet written. Most likely Paul never read any of the gospel stories. When Paul spoke about the gospel, he meant the power of personal experience, the "good news" of what happened to him when he met Christ. Paul was not ashamed of the gospel, (the "good news" he experienced) because it was this "good news" that was the power of God unto man's salvation.

The church must create an atmosphere conducive to individual participation in the work of the kingdom. The present approach of the church to soul winning is almost anti-New Testament. There was no church of this nature in the New Testament. They had preachers and a congregation, but there were no buildings. It was not the norm for all to go to one place, sit down and let one person stand up and speak. Even the eleven stood up while Peter preached. It has been suggested that there were no places to sit. Could it be that they had something in their hearts that would not let them sit idly by and not become involved in the message? Could it be that the inner "go ye" motivated them to total involvement?

A recent article in an airline magazine entitled, "Between Standing Up and Lying Down," says that all of the ills of the human family can be traced to the sitting position. Man was made to stand up and work until he got tired and then to lie down and rest until he was able to work again. People ask, why then is man physiologically permitted to sit down? The article answered that it was for versatility so man could move and work, but man misuses his versatility to sit down. Something about the sitting position alters the pressure on all of the vital organs of the body and causes most of man's physical problems. Perhaps it causes spiritual problems too.

The church is not supposed to be in a seated position. The New Testament Church was made up of men in motion. No provision was made for men to sit down until their work was finished. The very atmosphere of a church where everybody slips in, slumps down, sings, sleeps and slips out is contrary to basic New Testament Christianity.

The church that permits everyone to sit on the premises while singing, "Standing on the Promises" fails to create a New Testament atmosphere. So if the church pew is here to stay, the minister must effect "a spiritual revolution" and stir the people to stand on the ramparts and shout from the housetops, the message of Jesus.

The church must begin with New Testament means, the gospel, the power of God experienced personally through individual lives. This will produce New Testament men. Only New Testament means can produce New Testament men. Genesis declares: "The seed is in the fruit." Monkeys reproduce monkeys, sunflowers produce sunflower seeds, humans bear humans and Christians reproduce Christians. If the seed is not in the fruit, it is probably a hybrid variety that can never reproduce. Fruit without seeds may be good to eat, but without reproduction they are an end in themselves.

The church is producing a new kind of high-brow sophisticated Christianity that produces professing Christians who do not have the seed of the fruit in their hearts. The fruit of the Spirit is love, and the by-products of love are joy, peace, longsuffering, gentleness, faith, meekness and temperance. But love is not the fruit of a Christian. The showing of love, is demonstrating the fruit of the Spirit. When love is present, joy and peace are available. This is still the fruit of the Spirit. Christian fruit bearing is soul-winning, reproducing another Christian. The fruit of the Christian is another Christian.

So it is evident that New Testament men are produced only by New Testament means. New Testament methods alone could never produce New Testament men. The Jehovah's Witnesses and the Mormons use New Testament methods. The Fuller Brush man uses a New Testament method. Avon uses a New Testament method. Personalized methods alone do not produce New Testament men. Men may go two by two into every city and into every house declaring what they believe to be truth. They may use a New Testament method, but this alone will not produce New Testament men. New Testament means is the place to begin. To start with methods is definitely the wrong order. The church must begin with the gospel that transforms the individual into the life of a converted believer, then through this personal experience produce New Testament men. These men will feel comfortable using New Testament methods. Only then can the church grow.

Men concoct all kind of paraphernalia and programming to cover up weaknesses. Adequate programming is essential. The church must be organized and programmed. A structured and organized effort is imperative, but it must be structured within a New Testament framework and it must be based on the Word of God. All programs must feel natural to the worker. A TV advertisement by a manufacturer of hand tools "listens" to an arm work so the company can make hand tools fit the man. When the tool fits the hand, the man is happier and his work is more correct and he gets more production. Local churches that are doing the most good are the ones that have simple, understandable programs that the people can take and tailor just a little to fit their particular or unique need. The workers end up feeling as if the program is "our program." Having made the tool fit their hand, they feel comfortable using it.

Only New Testament men can adequately operate New Testament methods to produce more New Testament men. The New Testament cycle goes on. When the cycle is broken, a lot of people run around doing many things but accomplishing very little. A lot of noise is made: there is much sounding off and the blowing of trumpets, but not many people listen or respond. There is no communication. The essential New Testament atmosphere does not exist. To continue growing, the church must communicate. The Christian heritage must be taught to the next generation. Teaching that it is Christ-centered and New Testament related is essential to stability and progress. The heritage of the past must be applied to the present with implications for the future.

Teaching the Word is communicating experiential knowledge in a way others clearly understand. Communication is the shortest distance between a question in the mind of an inquirer and an answer experienced from the life and language of the New Testament. The story facts of the gospel do not change, but the frame of reference and the basic experience of people change with each generation. Each person is a child of his own age and culture. This complicates the communication of experiential knowledge and often leaves a great fixed gap between the pulpit and the pew.

Since teaching the Word is basic to evangelism, communicating the "good news" of personal experience is the inescapable work of the church. The facts of the Bible must be conducted in the framework of personal experience and linked with the kindred goals of evangelism. Converts to the Christian faith are made by the Word experienced in the life of others. Thus, it is obvious that Christians ought to be evangelistic in their daily lives. Born-again believers are the textbooks of evangelism and each Christian must become convert-conscious. When living gives priority to learning, the effectiveness of a Christian has its basis in understanding the spiritual needs of others.

Human efforts and effective methods are sure to fail without the element of personal experience to validate the invitation. The New Testament program works only if it is understood. The best way to understand the story facts of the gospel is to experience the reality of the living God personally and share these experienced truths with others.

Men are God's methods. Men transformed by the New Testament dynamic, become a means to reach others because of their personal relationship with Christ. Personal experience and first-hand evidence that the Word of God really works is the power that advanced the New Testament Church. This power of personal experience expressed in forceful and friendly witness is the means to propagate the Christian faith today and bring about genuine New Testament growth within the church.

4.

Programming
Limits
Mobilization

New Testament programming was simple. Extension sanctuaries in the home seemed to be a basic New Testament plan. "Where two or three are gathered together in my name, there am I." Where two or three were gathered together in Christ's name, the church happened. The Lord started with two—the nucleus—man and wife. He added three for the first child, because the child ought to be involved. The living room should be a room for life. "Daily in the temple and in every house they ceased not to teach and preach Jesus Christ." New Testament believers lived the life they preached.

To mobilize a congregation for Christian action there must be some structure, some organization to guide the people in their "going." This cannot be left to chance because programming requires understanding. The details of the New Testament program are not available. The Spirit gives only a glimpse into the concept. The Temple was a place of prayer. After prayer the leaders taught and preached. Not only in the Temple, which was a gathering place for religious people, but those who prayed also taught and preached in every house. Not that they went from house to house knocking on doors, but the people who went to the Temple to pray were going back to their own homes to teach, to preach and to live Christ. In every house where there was a Christian, there was teaching and witnessing. Not that the Apostles were in every house, but every believer in his own home was "having church."

Programming is important, but the kind of program the Apostles had is not fully known. They led people to the Temple for prayer and encouraged everyone to live right in their homes. That was program enough. Organized choirs, educational buildings and other programs may be helpful now, but seemed to be unnecessary in New Testament days. The church was everywhere. The program was understood because everyone was involved. All the people were mobilized for action.[4]

The pages of the New Testament do not exhort individuals or churches to provide money for the propagation of the faith. Neither does it constantly promote a program of outreach. The New Testament is concerned more with defining the faith and personal involvement. The writers of the New Testament do not feel the necessity to repeat the Great Commission or to urge that it is a duty of converts to go to every nation. The making of disciples seems to come as a natural sequence to conversion. The New Testament tells that the church was established in the faith and increased in number daily and in every place their faith was spread abroad. As believers were scattered abroad, they went everywhere witnessing to the grace of God.

History bears out that following the New Testament age, the Christian Church continued to expand and grow throughout the known world. There was a spontaneous expansion based on the effect the gospel had on individual converts. It was often the unorganized activity of individual members that expanded the gospel into the regions beyond. This is not to decry organization or formalized effort. It is simply to point out that New Testament Christians, spontaneously through the very nature of their conversion, become involved in effective outreach.

The act of accepting Christ seems to be an instinctive force which drives men even at the risk of life itself, to impart to others a new-found joy. It is not surprising then, that when Christians were scattered by persecution and Providence that there was a craving for fellowship and a demand for witness. Thus, a gospel outreach and an experience of power was effective in the winning of souls. Christians have a basic instinct for expression. There is a divine desire to share the "good news" of salvation with others and the Spirit always opens a free course of opportunity for witness.

Spontaneous outreach begins with the personal effort of individual Christians to assist their fellowman in understanding the nature of the "good news." The Christian experience is personal in nature. At times it even seems to have the force of a secret: it must be told. Even though it is told inadequately, it still excites and directs the individual to self activity: that of confessing sins and proclaiming the joy of salvation.

When an individual speaks voluntarily and spontaneously it has great effect upon those who hear. Not only does it affect the hearer, it also renews the past experience and revitalizes the individual who witnesses. Outreach begins with the individual witness and proceeds to corporate expression as the individual becomes an effective arm of evangelism. Roland Allen claims the "rapid and wide expansion" of the New Testament Church and the growth of the church "in the early century was due mainly to the spontaneous activity" of personal witness. Spontaneous zeal, the personal enthusiasm of a soul set afire by conversion and anointed by the Holy Spirit, is the great and perhaps the only force for church growth and the advancement of Christianity.[5]

A church expands simply by organizing these individuals into groups as they are converted and thereby directing their zeal toward the unsaved community and guiding them to understanding the knowledge of the faith and basic concepts of the New Testament. This spontaneous activity of the individual, within the group of which it is a part, stimulates and advances the whole cause of the church. The outreach ministry of the church when reduced to the basic elements is very simple, it requires no elaborate organization, no large expenses, and no great amount of paper work. The only prerequisite seems to be people in touch with God and in touch with their fellow-man.

The basic need for church advance is a genuine convert supplied by the Holy Spirit and pointed in the direction of need. There must be a simple organization based on the Word of God that places all men in right order with each other and in the proper relationship with God. All that is required is the basic faith in Christ and that the witness be led by the Spirit. Those who encourage individual Christian witness must be certain that the tools are natural to the person and that he feels comfortable within the framework and structure of the organized effort. If this is not true, then this outreach will be stifled and individual initiative will be curtailed and the growth of the church will be retarded.

One of the major obstacles in the advancement of the Christian faith is the misconception that ministers and missionaries are a special breed and alone have a call to evangelism. The New Testament is filled with incidents where new converts immediately plunged into the work of evangelism. A classic example is the story of the woman at the well who left her water pot and went on her way into the city and witnessed to the miraculous power of Christ; the whole city turned out to see Jesus. Some believed because of her testimony and others believed because of His words. Christ felt compelled to go through Samaria. His objective was to reach this woman with the message of living water. The scheme was to win one woman and through her win many of her acquaintances, relatives and fellow citizens including enemies.

Christ laid the foundation of a significant soul-saving work in all Samaria. At Jacob's Well the woman left her water pot. She was not told to go, she was not commissioned or commanded, yet the transformation within her compelled her to tell others to come and drink of the living water. Her witness precipitated a large-scale awakening in the city. The whole city responded to the woman's witness. In two days nearly the whole city was convinced that Christ was truly the Son of God.

A human chain reaction was set off in the streets of Jerusalem on the day of Pentecost. It is yielding energy, causing further reaction for the blessings of mankind, even to this day. One successive stage was demonstrated in Thessalonica, the capital of Macedonia. They received the Word and immediately "their faith was spread abroad" and "they sounded out the Word." What happened to the church in Thessalonica in ancient Greece is to be regarded as a precedent with believing nationals pulsatingly aware that the commission included them. Because of their evangelistic energies, Paul considered this Greek church to be a pattern for all Gentile believers. Christians need to see their faith as a precious thing, designed to be shared and to understand that when it is not sent abroad it deteriorates at home. When Christians today follow the New Testament example of the Thessalonians, the Christian witness will take a great leap forward toward the goal of winning the world.

However, church growth problems will persist as long as the church attempts to perpetuate programs that are complicated and ineffectual. The more difficult a program is to understand the fewer persons will be motivated by it. Without total motivation there can be no complete mobilization. Complicated methods and overprogramming limits mobilization because the congregation does not understand. When the programs fail, often the personnel are blamed. Consequently, the church becomes imprisoned by previous patterns and perpetuates unworkable programs. The key to growth is simple programming that everyone can understand and in which everyone can become involved.

5.

Church
Is Imprisoned
by Previous Patterns

It is obvious that the church has become imprisoned by the patterns of previous generations. In an effort to perpetuate the sameness of doctrine that is called "the faith of our fathers," the church attempts to perpetuate the same programs as well. Although it is not necessary to change theologically, programs must be changed to meet the needs of contemporary society. It is not the lack of change *per se* that makes the difference, it is whether or not the programs of the church are contemporary. In fact, it is not new programs that are needed, it is the simple concepts of the New Testament in operation in the daily lives of each member. It is the hangover programs from the "hell fire and brimstone" generation that seems to be cloging up the works. This is evident in the kind of motivation necessary to get people involved.

Basically, there are three kinds of motivation: (1) push motivation—which uses fear as its force; (2) pull motivation—which uses incentive and rewards; and (3) personal motivation by love. When Christians have to be pushed or pulled into participation or involvement in the program of the church, it should be obvious that something is wrong with both the program and the Christian.

One of the problems seems to be that most church members feel they have secured a "fire insurance policy" that guarantees eternal life so there is little need to become involved or to worry with the earthly state of the church. Their concern seems to be to stay out of trouble and to remain at least on the list of "saints who have never been caught." The result is that they become inactive with almost no involvement in the ongoing program of the church. There seems to be no personal incentive for involvement.

A genuine Christian experience should be sufficient to give one a personal incentive for participating in the program of the church. Conversion should cause the convert to change direction and become involved in life in a new and creative way. This involvement would include participation in things which open the doors for evangelism and Christian education and the improvement of the earthly lot of all men.

The prison of previous patterns seems to operate according to the law of inertia. Some persons established in the way seem to be stuck and immovable. On the other hand, there seem to be others who are hyperactive and committed to full involvement in the multiplicity of church programming. The first group is satisfied with things as they are. The second group is happy only when they are in motion and willingly settle for motion without actual progress.

Involvement without results and motion without progress leads to emotional and spiritual exhaustion without worthwhile accomplishments. The life of the church becomes monotonous and boring because it is routine, regular and very similar to running on a treadmill. Everyone is busy, the church calendar is full, the weekly cycle has a planned program every night, there is a rapid succession of drives and promotions that never seem to accomplish anything. Special days are there to be celebrated, attended or promoted but no real meaning for the Christian life seems to emerge from these observances. Banquets, dinners, cookouts, funerals, weddings, workshops and seminars, compete for the physical presence of the body but offer very little intellectual stimulation or emotional satisfaction.

Accepting the prison of previous patterns forced upon each succeeding generation by their elders, seems to cause an adjustment to mediocrity. The endless routine of activities that have little meaning overwhelm the people by demanding their time and presence until there is nothing left for the spiritual life of the church. An automatic and superficial response to the needs of the people develops. The vision of the congregation dims and the spirit wilts. Slowly the programs and opportunities that once held a promise of fulfillment become a burden and a drudgery. Everyone attends out of loyalty but there is no real personal motivation by love that would demand a meaningful involvement.

The tragedy of such busyness is that much energy and good talent goes to waste that could be channeled by the Holy Spirit into real New Testament ministry. There are many Martha's who want to stay busy in honest labor and very few Mary's who are willing to spend a few moments at the Master's feet (Luke 10:38-42). Christ did not condemn Martha's labor of love but He did state that Mary's seemingly idle moments were the better choice. Actually, by spending a few moments at the Master's feet, Mary could have a much more meaningful involvement in the normal activities of life.

Oftentimes the church that keeps people "on the go" day and night has confused the priorities of the Commission. The "going" was to be automatic, the program was to be the "making of disciples" and initiating them into the fellowship and work of God. The church program now seems to be preoccupied with the secondary—that of building buildings, advancing programs, supporting personalities and practicing for some "future event." Even a great deal of the worship service is given to the performing arts and the promotion of programs that are to take place in the future.

All of this seems to be imprisoning the church in previous patterns and robbing them of the present reality of simple and sincere worship. It is definitely involving them in the wrong kind of activity and in the wrong kind of program. Certainly, it is a labor of love but the better part seems to be spending some time at the Master's feet.

Perhaps one reason ministers run on the treadmill of churchly busyness is that they feel insecure. The fledgling preacher who does not dare pause in his breathless delivery is an example. Should he stop he is afraid he would not know how to continue. The pastor may be avoiding solitude and time for reflection for fear of having to acknowledge to himself his inadequacies which he knows are there. Staying busy becomes an escape or a cover-up.

Pressures to succeed may be another contributing factor to the treadmill syndrome prevalent today. In the church success comes all too often in terms of rising attendance figures or financial gain. In such a climate where greater emphasis is given to quantity than to quality, numbers soon become the reason for ministry rather than the result. Since numbers are produced with an endless parade of promotions and church-centered activities, the pastor relentlessly drives himself and his congregation to produce more impressive statistics.

To be released from the prison of previous patterns, several steps could prove helpful. First, there needs to be a fresh awareness that the ministry is a spiritual enterprise and that its accomplishments must come primarily through spiritual means. The word of the Lord to Zerubbabel through the prophet Zechariah is applicable to today's kingdom tasks as well: "Not by might, nor by power, but by my spirit, saith the Lord of hosts" (Zechariah 4:6).

Secondly, a clear reaffirmation of discipleship to Christ will help the minister to establish again a proper roster of priorities and to resist the temptation to serve man's interests rather than God's. Also, through a renewed commitment to his Lord, the minister may discover that he does not need to hide his insecurity in frantic activity. Instead he may find that he is able to enter into a relaxed but steady improvement with God and His work. Perchance he will also find the courage to say "no" to the trivial and the unreasonable.

A good way to break the pattern of the past is to stop the "hurry, worry" approach to life. The minister who is willing to reflect and take stock of his work and accomplishments has taken the first steps toward liberating himself once more for the meaningful pursuit of his high calling. He can also lead his people into meaningful worship and practical involvement in the work of the kingdom.[6]

6.

Base Becomes
the Field
of Operations

When the building complex and the church constituency become the field in which to work rather than a force with which to work, the church is in trouble. Admittedly, a program of Christian growth and development is essential in the training of the young and in the instruction of new converts. The church is to be a base for operations and not the field in which to do all the work. Perhaps the church should get back to the New Testament pattern and follow the simple plan of evangelism used by the earliest followers of Christ.

The basic premise undergirding the advance of Christianity is that the church must accept responsibility for carrying the message of Christ to people outside the four walls of the church building. Since "church growth depends on the winning of converts," [7] and it is evident that ministry within the church alone can never reach the masses, Christians must be concerned about converts from the community. Too long the ministry of evangelism has been limited within the building complex and the present church constituency. It is time for the church to build bridges of outreach, not walls of isolation.

Church ministries should be designed to expand the church beyond the building complex and take the message of saving grace to the community. Church extension enables leadership to generate spiritual enthusiasm for active participation in Christ's Commission and involves the whole Christian family in God's plan of reaching, teaching, winning and developing. It gives an essential motivation to "Go out into the highways and hedges and urge and constrain them to yield and come in, so that my house may be filled [with worshipers]" (Luke 12:43 ANT). The church growth emphasis is dual: the multitudes outside the church must be reached with the Christian gospel and the unlimited power of the Holy Spirit must be appropriated to enable the church to accomplish this task.

The church was not born to be a hospital for saints or a social club for sinners. Its very existence indicates God's purpose: to evangelize the world. The gates of hell shall not prevail against God's church because it is God's primary instrument for winning the world. God gave, Christ gave and the Spirit was given to man to enable him to give of his best to the Lord's work. God is not willing that any should perish but His desire is that all men come to a saving knowledge of His Son and become involved in the fellowship of the church.

The church is not sent to save the world, the community, or the family; her mission is to bring the saving gospel to individuals. The Spirit of God deals with the world, the community, and the church usually in groups to prepare the way for the Word of God. The Word then speaks to individuals. Men are born one at a time and they must be born again one at a time. This suggests a dangerous misconception about "mass" evangelism. Actually, "mass" evangelism is a misnomer. What happens is "simultaneous soul winning" or "multi-individual" decisions. Evangelism is actually personal in nature.

Great waves of revival have circled the globe, but for the most part the personal and practical aspects of evangelism have not been truly understood. The true elements of soul winning were lost in the popularity of the preacher and in the vastness of the congregation. Preachers still journey from church to church rather than house to house. Churchmen attempt to reverse the New Testament pattern by inviting everyone to one place so they can be saved rather than taking the gospel to where the people are. In such cases, the base of operation becomes the field of operation.

Less than five percent of Christians, according to a Moody Bible Institute estimate, have ever led a soul to Christ. It has also been estimated that no more than ten percent of the English-speaking population of the world attend church during their lifetime and this attendance is less that regular or systematic. If this be true, at least ninety percent of the unsaved people will never enter a church except for a funeral or a wedding. This means that the gospel must be lived before them and taken to them through individuals.

There is no command in the Scriptures for sinners to go the house of God, yet there are explicit instructions for believers to "make disciples" as they go into all the world. Yet the only thing that most Christians know about the heathen who are lost are the pictures taken by some ghetto minister for an inner city project or the slides presented by the typical "missionary on furlough." Some seem to paraphrase the Great Commission to read: "Go ye into all the world and take a picture of every creature." [8] Somehow a mysterious idea prevails that heathen whose picture is captured by a Christian's camera is to be eternally saved.

When the church walls itself in and ministers only to those who attend, the base becomes the field of operation. This drastically, if not entirely, limits the outreach of the church. A program of structured outreach by a group may be effective, but an unstructured effort based on individual initiative and inner motivation is often the thing that really works. The preaching of the gospel, the teaching of the Word, the singing of hymns, the praying and the Christian fellowship in the church should create a force to send the membership into the whitened fields of harvest.

Christians constantly are coming together. When they scatter following a worship service, for the most part they are not indentifiable as a church. The harvest is great, but the laborers are few. A ripened harvest of souls waits to be reaped. Christ-like men ought to be moved with compassion at the multitudes who are scattered abroad as sheep having no shepherd.

Evangelism was never intended to be carried on inside the church building. Only a few who are lost enter the sanctuary at the time of worship or on special occasions. Evangelism is something that must be done outside the four walls of the church where the sinners are. The church building may be a place for revival and a place where believers come to be nourished up in the faith, taught the doctrines of the Word, and strengthened as believers. But soul winning, for the most part, is done outside the church sanctuary. The church at worship is a meeting of those already won. The gathering is to instruct, to experience, so they may in turn become effective witnesses for Christ. Believers are to go forth into the community witnessing and winning those who are lost. Unless the church quickly reinstitutes the concept of individual witness, the lost world can never be won.

Laborers are few in the field of personal soul winning because most Christian service takes place within the framework of the structured church. Their energies are expended singing in the choir, teaching in the program of Christian education or directing youth activities. All the activity takes place within "God's little acre." There are almost no laborers in the harvest field.

Today the church has nearly lost the concept of being Christian because it necessitates a concern for the personal and family needs of others. Christians regularly worship in beautiful sanctuaries with little or no concern for the sinners in the streets. Since sinners usually do not come to the church sanctuary, it seems very futile to make the base of operation also the field of operations.

Unless Christians rush quickly into the world and stake a fervent claim for Christ, the world is hopelessly lost. Sinners may never be churched, but many of them could be converted and brought to a saving knowledge of Christ if they were told the simple story of Jesus' love.

The early church understood their commission as Christians. Not only the Apostles, but each believer knew he was to be a daily witness to the saving grace. Daily in houses, on the streets, at the well, in the markets, on the roadways and in the fields they preached Christ and won souls. They knew Christ was living and would some day return. They told everyone the "good news" until almost every person in the "then known world" knew that a man named Jesus Christ had lived, died and that many believed He had risen from the dead.

The church has become more interested in conserving things already attained than pressing forth into the world with the good news. Consequently, the base has become the field of operation. When conventions, seminars and workshops replace personal evangelism, decay and deterioration has begun. When the splitting of theological hairs overshadows the personal experience of believers, the Christian mission to all the world is in jeopardy. When believers lose the hope of eternal life and the imminent return of Christ for His people, the church sleeps, becomes lethargic and neglects the awesome responsibility of reaching out for the lost.

God has constantly thrust the church forth into the community. Following the outpouring of the Spirit at Pentecost pilgrims and travelers returned home with news of what happened in Jerusalem. The doctrine spread. A short time later, however, the Christians in Jerusalem became satisfied with making their Jerusalem base the field of operation. The force for operation had been limited to those already won. It was through the hand of Saul of Tarsus that God stirred up the nest of the Jerusalem Christians and scattered them abroad throughout the land so they could see more clearly the individual responsibility for effective personal witnessing. Men of God, dedicated men, still stand in the bell tower pulling the rope and listening to the bell say, "Come to worship, come to worship," when the message of the New Testament rings clear, "Go out into the highways and hedges . . . go into all the world . . . go to every creature."

Jesus Christ preached perhaps His greatest sermons and made some of His most profound statements to individuals such as Nicodemus or the Samaritan woman at the well. Philip, an early evangelist, took a long journey to minister to one individual soul in the desert. Paul preached to such individuals as Felix the Governor and King Agrippa, yet today, ministers of the gospel feel they must have a large crowd before they can "give their best."

When Paul, as an early church leader, told young Timothy to do the work of an "evangelist," he was not suggesting that this young man conduct protracted meetings or a series of special services. He was saying: "You are not only a preacher, a teacher, a leader of men, you are also a soul winner." Personally, individually, Timothy was to tell the good news. He was to become a daily crusader for souls. He was to be a personal witness of the message he preached—a product of the product.

Only when the preacher himself can go into the streets and the lanes of the city and be a personal witness for Christ can he adequately lead the congregation into New Testament evangelism. Regretfully, many men of God cannot adequately present the claims of Christ to the lost. They spend much time arranging and preparing programs to get others to attempt to do what they do not have the inspiration or the spiritual "go ye" to do. For the most part, the clergy has failed as "apostles of the streets."

Church life must be based on penetrating Biblical insights. Theology, worthy of the name in any context, is intensely practical and personal. Theology today, to be effective, must have the living interaction of Biblical revelation. Men cannot domesticate God. Nor can they require His presence in Sunday services or His blessings upon a particular ecclesiastical colony of a specific local "gospel ghetto" when they in fact deny His effective work in the community. Evangelism can take place in and through the church only when men cease their futile efforts to control and regulate the Spirit and allow the Spirit to anoint them and thrust them forth into a needy world. The church does not manage the commission. The Holy Spirit, through conversion, commission and commitment, directs the only adequate program of the church in the world.

A strategy of penetration includes the individual operation of saints. Peter was given the keys to the kingdom and the followers of Christ were compared with salt and light. Salt can penetrate and preserve. Light can penetrate and illuminate. The church has the capacity to penetrate the lock that has fenced in the church and walled out the world. Each individual Christian has a capacity to penetrate the society of which he is a part. Christ came to cause fire upon the earth, but fire continues only as long as it has new fuel. Thus, the strategy of penetration requires continuous addition of fuel. New converts must be won and brought into the church as worshipers.

The problem of the Sunday-oriented congregation limited to the building facility is of major consequence to church growth. It is important to understand that the earliest congregation owned no buildings. They were so deeply engaged in the task of penetrating the world they did not have time to erect monuments or count the results of their efforts. The oldest known Christian structures date from about 250 A.D. and those were underground at Rome. When Christians did finally begin to build, most of their buildings were normally the house-type dwelling rather than the shrine. They were basically house churches (I Corinthians 16:19; Colossians 4:15). If the church building complex can be the base of operation and the community can be the field in which to work, then the two can go together. But when the church building facility becomes both the base and the field, a serious problem of church growth is evident.

7.

Congregation Is Unaware of Dying Organism

As man grows older, some parts of the body stop working. An eye quits, a leg gives out, a finger stops. Exercise, vitamins, medical care, and a multiplicity of other things come into the picture to prolong the vitality of the body. A basic human desire is to remain young and active. No one wants to get old until he does; then he wants to get as old as he can. Even incapacity and sickness are usually preferred to death. As long as there is a spark of life and consciousness, man wants to live.

This points to a serious church growth problem because a similar attitude exists concerning many aspects of the church. The church is permitted to age, mature and become bound by tradition. No one is willing to let the "old ways" die. Consequently, the tradition continues. The machinery is maintained even though the church loses relevance and cannot communicate. Yet, most congregants are unaware that the church is dying.

Scientists speak of all living things as organisms. A human being is an organism—so is a mouse, a fish, an insect or a worm; so is a tree, a daisy, or a fungus; so are bacteria and other tiny creatures. Any living thing is an organism. The church is classified as a living substance. Christ is the Head with the whole Body fitly framed together. Christ is the Head whether the church is considered the Body or the Bride. Thus, the church is usually considered to be a spiritual organism.

An organism has organization. All living things share some important features. The very word "organism" suggests that each living thing is organized. That is, its parts are arranged in certain ways and do certain work within the organism. No matter how simple an organism appears to be, it is very highly organized. Nothing is more organized than the human body. Have you noticed how regularly your body functions? Have you noticed how organized your body is? How systematized God made the body?

The church is an organism and God has regulated and organized the church. Churchmen must work on both parts of the church: the organism and the organization. Church growth does not necessarily come from working on the organization, but comes from perfecting the organism: the spiritual life of the church. Church growth then can be maintained by working on the organization. In this respect organization is vital to continued vitality.

A church must have a system of organization. It should not be overly organized but it should have organization. To overly discipline the body with exercise causes sore muscles. When the organizational rules are broken, it causes trouble. The church has both life and organization, but it is possible for the organism to die and the organization remain. Organizations can never give life to a dead organism. Only God can provide the spark of life.

There is a spiritual quality and a physical quality to the church. Some things which the church desperately needs done, God will not do. Other things, only God can do for the church. God is not going to shovel the snow off the sidewalk or change a lightbulb when it burns out. Some things men must do to keep the organization functioning. The human body is the best scientifically organized machine in the whole world, but unless it is fed it will be just as the automobile—it will run out of fuel. Man cannot work only on one side and neglect the other.

Some are concerned about the spiritual side of the church and the physical side is neglected, or vice versa.

An organism not only has organization but it also has activity and energy. Organization does not in itself make a substance live. To be alive a substance must be active. The activity of an organism is chemical and it takes place inside the organism. This chemical activity is a continuous process without which the organism would not be alive. Energy must continually enter the organism so that the invisible living machinery keeps going. Without energy there can be no activity. It is not just activity, it is activity produced by inner energy. In an organism it is called chemical action that brings about action. In the church, spiritual energy brings about the action. It is spiritual, internal motivation! The Spirit motivates men to work on the organism to keep the organization alive. No amount of external stimuli can adequately motivate the church to true Christian action.

An organism has both shape and substance. New material is continually flowing into the substance to alter the shape. New elements take the place of older material which is continually being pushed out or used up. This process alters both shape and substance.

The appearance of the church building is not the shape of the church. A church is not shaped as a square or a rectangle. The true shape of a church appears more as a city map, because a church is shaped by the community. Those who gather at the meeting place are the substance, the essential nature of the church. The shape of the church has something to do with the shape of the community. The substance of the church is determined by the actual membership. The substance and the surroundings determine the shape of the church.

Living material changes continually. An organism grows when new material flows in faster than the old material moves out. As long as an organism is increasing in size or weight, it is growing. This process of change and growth constantly goes on within an organism. All growth is temporary. Change must come, because growth produces change. Sometimes the change is for good. Growth always produces change but change does not necessarily produce growth. The church must never change the essential nature given by God but the church must be willing to become relevant to each new generation or stop growing.

An organism has the power of reproduction. In all living things the process of reproduction makes small, new organisms, which replace larger, older organisms; otherwise life would disappear. When the female no longer is able to bear a child she has reached a critical point in her life. She is still a woman, still a wife and still a mother, but she no longer has the capacity to produce children. This causes many problems. When a woman reaches this stage prematurely, the problems are more acute.

The church is classified as a woman in Scripture. The church must be understood as a female organism. "There are sons ready to be born, but not strength to bring them forth." This condition would certainly be tragic. Is the church too weak to give birth to sons that are ready to be born? An understanding of these difficulties helps to visualize the problems of the church. A living organism has the power of reproduction and when it loses that power it is getting old. When a woman loses her power of reproduction she must concentrate on other things: being a wife to her husband, and a mother to her children, or adopt a child.

Pastors faced with this problem must decide if they are satisfied with the size of the church and be a good pastor of the sheep he has or find another way to acquire members. Does the church have the capacity to go out in the community to win others? Paul could say "I was the man involved, I worked with the church. I took the seed of the Word. I begat men with the gospel. I became a spiritual father." If the church does not have the strength to bear children, it must adopt. The alternative is clear: Go out in the highways and hedges and find those not in the church and get them into the house of the Lord as worshipers.

When the reproduction cycle is over and the life of the organism slows down, the aging process has begun. Then comes a disintegration and ultimately there would be death because all growth is temporary. Once an organism has become full size, it no longer grows. The flow of energy and matter continues, but it gradually slows down. Finally old material breaks down faster than new material builds up. The organism ages and finally fades away. Death is the end for every organism without a system of renewal. Old churches may not die, but they are certain to fade away, lose their Christian influence and cease to be adequate for the spiritual needs of the community. This is spiritual death.

The church is not a normal organism. The church is a divine institution as well as a spiritual organism. There will be faith on earth when Christ returns. The power of the Spirit is adequate to keep the church alive until Jesus comes for His bride. The death of the universal church will not come. There may be disintegrating parts of the church and men may see parts of the church die off, but the Church of Jesus Christ will ultimately be triumphant!

Preacher, Pews and Proselytes

(Personnel-Centered Problems)

Personnel-centered problems begin with the pulpit and the downgrading of proclamation. This causes the purpose of the church as the living Body of Christ to be thwarted. Consequently, a gap grows between the pulpit and pew producing weak links that endanger the chain of evangelism. Perhaps the most serious consequence of the weak pulpit is the preaching of cheap grace. This produces poor converts and causes the church to reach converts who have an intellectual apprehension of truth but often possess little experiential knowledge. Thus, the church has difficulty in leading the convert into an active life as a Christian disciple. When converts do not grow in grace and knowledge, it is impossible to produce believers who can be entrusted with the saving witness as "apostles of the streets."

8. Proclamation Is Downgraded
9. Purpose of the Church Is Thwarted
10. Growing Gap Between Pulpit and Pew Is Overlooked
11. Weak Links Endanger the Chain of Evangelism
12. Cheap Grace Produces Poor Converts
13. Converts Do Not Become Disciples
14. Disciples Do Not Become Apostles

8.

Proclamation
Is
Downgraded

Preaching is the proclamation of the Word of God to men by men anointed of God. Yet proclamation is being downgraded even though the people are still willing to listen. Much of the fault is in the sender and not in the receiver. The problem is not to get the hungry to eat. The problem is to provide sufficient food nutritious enough to meet his needs. A convention of farmers and ranchers would never spend time on "how to get a cow to come to the barn" or "how to get a cow to eat." The program would probably concern itself with improving the feed to take advantage of the appetite that always exists.

This is a far cry from what takes place at a conference for ministers. When the clergy concentrates on "improving the feed" and makes an effort to build stronger pulpits, the congregation will gladly and eagerly listen to the Word of God. The people will sense in the man of God the spirit of Jeremiah who spoke for every preacher, "his word was in mine heart as a burning fire. . . ."

There is little reason for the church to congregate unless there is a strong pulpit personality with a distinctive message to challenge and inspire them to return.

Many people with problems attend church earnestly and sincerely seeking answers but are disappointed. The answers are in the Word of God. Many problems remain unresolved because the clergy is so involved in the intricate details of regulating religious machinery and oiling ecclesiastical programs that little time is given to the Word. The church for years was able to maintain its position in society with a minimum effort toward sermon excellence because laymen were reluctant to criticize. This has caused many clergymen to drift through the week riding on a crest of compliments and prestige and neglecting adequate sermon preparation. He is expected to have a message direct from God; a message to challenge and inspire the hearts of men. Very few deliver such a sermon. It is no wonder why busy men, families with problems or young people searching for answers do not return.

Pickett declares preaching to be "a vital function" of the Christian Church.[9] The New Testament Church was involved in many activities but proclamation always had priority; it was never relegated to a secondary position. Paul told Timothy, "I was ordained a preacher." In the letter to the Romans, Paul made it clear that man cannot hear without a preacher and that faith comes from what he had heard from a preacher. Men will still listen to a message from God.

A minister is primarily a preacher. He may be called upon to be a counselor, administrator and many other things, but his primary task is that of delivering the Word of God. Each clergyman must remember: "It pleased God by the foolishness of preaching to save them that believed" (I Corinthians 1:21).

The work of the church is to provide the Word. It is the Word that provides strength for the journey. It may be received from a pulpit, a printing press, by the witness of a friend or through a personal devotion. Many forms and different methods may be used, but it is still the proclamation of the Word that furnishes the necessary strength and energy for Christian living and effective witnessing.

A minister must not come to a worship service excusing his lack of preparation and spiritual depth on a busy schedule and the problems of running the organization. What would happen to the surgeon who entered the operating room unprepared? What action would take place if the school teacher or college professor were to neglect the necessary preparation? How long can preachers get by with less than adequate preparation for the pulpit?

All of the social involvements and intellectual pursuits of the minister will not satisfy the hungry people looking for the Bread of Life. The church may embellish the table settings and employ highly trained chefs and winsome waiters but the people suffer spiritual malnutrition because the table too often is empty of basic foods. This is the greatest lack in the church. There are ample administrators and the church has enough social leaders and plenty of program promoters but there is a desperate need for the exhorting "pulpiteers" of yesteryear.

A focus on the minister's calling and task points to him as a man of God who speaks the Word of the Lord. Preaching and teaching are linked in many ways, but preaching is to have priority. Preaching is not to be talk about Christianity; it is to be a message about God's acts. The important question is not whether the sermon starts with a passage of scripture but whether what the preacher says as a whole is the gospel or not. Men of the cloth must remember that it is not the preacher who preaches; it is the Holy Spirit who proclaims God's Word in the words of the preacher.

The problem of preaching is often the preacher. The minister is derelict in his responsibility unless he comes to the pulpit and speaks with one purpose: to bring about an encounter between the people and the Word of God. The church stands between the times: between God's decisive victory on the Cross and the final consummation. God seeks to speak to His people but often the preacher is more concerned about himself than about God's speaking His Word to His people. Instead of recounting and proclaiming the mighty acts of God, the preacher makes himself the center of attraction.

The Bible is the basis and the condition of all authentic preaching. Ministers must be men of one Book as well as of many books. When the preacher ceases to proclaim what God has done for man in Christ, he ceases to preach. The preacher is never sufficient within himself; no matter how thorough his exegesis, he must rely upon the Holy Spirit. Prayer may be the most difficult part of his preparation, but unless he is spiritually prepared he cannot become an instrument of proclamation. To enter the pulpit unprepared is to downgrade the proclamation of the gospel.

Pickett observes "preaching is not always verbal." [10] The daily life of the individual Christian is an open book that is read of all men. The witness is both in life and lip. In fact, the most effective witnessing is that proclamation by a dedicated life in the work-a-day world.

All the gospel writers present Christ as a preacher, but never only a preacher. Matthew, for example, says, "He went all about Galilee teaching and preaching and healing every disease and infirmity among the people." He clearly did not regard preaching as sufficient. He preached with authority, yet preaching alone was not enough. The works of Jesus confirmed His preaching in the life of the New Testament believers and confirmed their witness.

At least four of Christ's early disciples decided to assemble the records of what He said and did. These records are called the Gospels. The sermons of these disciples are forgotten, but their record of the life of Christ is read every day around the world. One of these disciples, Luke, wrote a second volume dealing chiefly with the rapid growth of the church. He told of the multitudes who declared their faith and were added to the fellowship of believers. He compared the ministry and labors of Peter (the chief preacher of the Jews) and Paul (the chief preacher of the Gentiles). He told of the rapid expansion and planting of many churches in Asia Minor and Greece. This record tells us that proclamation plus practical Christian living can be adequate in winning converts and planting churches.

Proclamation must have priority. Not necessarily pulpit preaching but proclamation: teaching, witnessing, declaring the "good news." The pulpit has its place, but somehow every believer must feel a responsibility to carry the "good news" everywhere. This must have priority in a program of growth in a local church. Unless proclamation of the "good news" has priority in the life of every believer the true purpose of the church will be thwarted.

9.

Purpose
of the Church
Is Thwarted

Why did Christ establish a church? On what basis did He establish it and for what purpose? Christ said, "Upon this rock I will build my church." Upon the profession of faith that He was the Son of God a church would be built. Christ would work through men such as Peter who had this faith and together they would assemble believers throughout the world to worship the true God and do His work among men. The church was to be Christ's Body reaching out to the needs of mankind.

God created man in His own image, but the partnership of man with God was broken by sin in the garden. Nevertheless, God's love continued. He selected a man and from this man He grew a family and a nation. This nation became a holy people and a kingdom of priests unto God and bore a Savior for mankind. This Savior lived and died, was buried and raised again, ascended to heaven and there continually intercedes in behalf of His followers on earth. The Holy Spirit through believers continues God's work in the world.

Christ said, "My Father worketh hitherto and I work and as the Father has sent me, so send I you." Through the church, God's partnership with man was resumed. The church, then, is direct evidence of human involvement in the divine plan and in the scheme of redemption for the world. This is the purpose of the church.

The New Testament Church was more than a congregation, more than a fellowship of redeemed people, it was a spiritual community. It was neither a building nor a hierarchy. It was a gathering of called-out people into a new kind of fellowship and community.[11] Christ was the head and although men were selected as leaders, the true life and leadership was from Christ. Christ purchased the church with His own blood. His death and resurrection assured spiritual vitality for the organized efforts of man. Any man who was to be "in Christ" was to be a new creation with an emphasis on *new*. The church was to bring a newness of life, a ministry of reconciliation and make men into ambassadors for Christ and partners with one another in extending the work of Christ in the world.

The life and vitality of the early church was made evident by the coming of the Holy Spirit at Pentecost.[12] A church today finds its present meaning and dynamics through Christ and the Holy Spirit. The function of an adequate church is obvious from history. Essential action of the church is worship, ministry, witness, Christian education, evangelism and the application of truth to life. Obviously, anything or anyone that hinders this essential action, greatly thwarts the purpose of the church.

The true purpose of the church can best be seen by taking an overview of its essence and function. The institution which often passes as the church is less than the church. The church is the sum of all true believers in Christ. Under the gospel, members of the church are distinguished because they let the mind be in them which was in Christ Jesus. It is a discipleship of commitment based on the example of Jesus. It is difficult to abstract from the Bible a definite measure of the true Christian in action. The Holy Scriptures do not set forth a neat blueprint, but it is clear that any lack of personal involvement thwarts the purpose of the church.

True, the church is people, but the church is more than people. It is people who have come together, who have made contact with and are acted upon by the gospel. To see people intimately involved in the church is to know that behind, beyond or above each of them lies something else that gives them their cohesiveness and force. That "something" is the gospel of Jesus Christ and the power of the Holy Spirit.

When the congregation is looked upon as the church, men see the church only as an organization of individuals without the enabling of the Holy Spirit or the commission of Christ. There is a difference between the appearance of things and the essence of things. The people are not the church, it is the power of God within man that brings men together, and when they are together in Christ, then and only then does the church happen, and it is God's church.

The reason the Scriptures do not tell us what a Christian is, is because a New Testament convert had the quality of becoming automatically that which he ought to be. The quality of the convert pressed the individual into Christian action. Therefore, the example of the believers in the Book of Acts points to a complete and total involvement in the witness of Christ's saving grace to the world.

In the New Testament the word most often used for church, Greek *ekklesia* (from a verb, call), can mean an assembly of persons for a particular purpose, religious or secular—even a spontaneous meeting (Acts 19:32, 40), as well as the various Christian Church meanings: church meeting, church or congregation in one place, the house churches, the church universal (all believers) plus local and universal church in such terms as "church of God," "church of Christ." Arndt-Gingrich calls this an "essentially Pauline usage."

Ekklesia was used 112 times in the New Testament but only once referred to a Hebrew congregation. This seems to give the New Testament Church a distinctive Gentile character. The New Testament Church was to be more than a *synagogue*, a gathering together of people. The Hebrew people knew they were the people of God. Daily personal and domestic regulations made this fact clear. They were a kingdom of priests with every family and each person a vital part of the whole nation. The Holy Spirit gave *ekklesia* a special meaning to Gentile believers. They were to be the church everywhere. The church was to be God's means to elicit worship and evoke witness.

To make this fact clear to the New Testament Church, the Spirit used *ekklesia*. This meeting of citizens was special, but was only part of the normal activities. All who met were citizens before, during and after the meeting. The coming together simply assisted them in becoming better citizens in a better city. The same is true of the church. Christians are a part of the church before, during and after the regularly scheduled meetings. The true Christian is always part of the church. A failure to see this complicates the clear understanding of the purpose of the church.

The English word *church* is usually considered to come from the Greek adjective *kuriakon*, originally used for "the Lord's House" and then for His people. Church in its ecclesiastical sense means that spiritual family of God, the communion (fellowship) of saints, those who have been brought to faith in Christ Jesus by the operation of the Holy Spirit. In this sense the church is not an institution but a divine creation. Christ is the Head of the Body, the church (Colossians 1:18). In another picture Christ is the Bridegroom; the church is the Bride. The church is also compared to a temple in which Christ is Foundation and Cornerstone (Ephesians 2:20-22).

The members of the church, "the called together by Christ," are ministered to be chosen members. "Ministry" as "church" has wider and narrower meanings. In the wider sense ministry includes every form of preaching or witnessing to the means of grace; to this every Christian is called. In the narrower sense ministry includes the public ministry of the means of grace which

Christians entrust to chosen public servants, who then serve on behalf of the whole congregation.

False views regarding the nature and purpose of the church include the idea that outward affiliation with a church ensures one's salvation. Strictly speaking, the Christian Church is made up of only those who believe and trust in Jesus as their personal Savior from sin. God in Christ has made them members of His communion of saints.

Then there are those who, in their wrong view of the church, would put the good works of the believers on the same level with the merit of Christ who died for the sins of the world. They would require the "observance of the commandments and of the church" for obtaining grace and salvation. However, when people trust their own good works for salvation, even partly, they are really excluding themselves from the grace of God and from membership in His church.

The altering of this concept has caused the major purpose of the church to become dim. As personnel become preoccupied with the ongoing details of program, conflicting purposes develop. An adequate diagnosis of the present difficulties is almost impossible. One thing however is certain. When the clergy, confronted with conflicting purposes, choose as their first and primary task, prayer and the ministry of the Word (Acts 6), other things will fall in place. As the spiritual needs of the congregation are met by dedicated ministers, the role of the laity in the work of God becomes increasingly clear. Anything less than complete personal involvement tends to thwart the progress of the church.

10.

Growing Gap
Between Pulpit and Pew
Is Overlooked

When the vividness necessary to motivate involvement is missing, the gap between pulpit and pew grows.[13] Maintaining things as they are becomes the actual purpose of the church. This over-institutionalization causes the church to exist to preserve itself rather than to be creatively involved in winning the world. As various leaders begin to promote a multiplicity of personally related causes, the will of the people to follow is replaced by a subdued antagonism. Personal incentives are lost. Inertia, discontent and conflict develops. The ensuing tension is a factor in the failure to maintain the purpose-centeredness of the contemporary church.

A growing gap exists between the pulpit and the pew basically because the work of equipping the saints is neglected. The special gifts of ministry were given to men that they may in turn equip others for Christian service and the upbuilding of the Body of Christ. The task of church leadership is simply one of equipping the saints for an effective ministry. It is obvious from the scripture that every believer is either in the process of being equipped himself, equipping others, or perhaps both. When man underestimates and ignores the power which God has given to the individual believer, he alienates himself from the spiritual equipment necessary to turn the tide of evil in this present world.

Lip service to the priesthood of believers widens the gap between the pulpit and the pew. Whether this is caused by weak ministry from the pulpit or false concepts in the congregation is not known. Perhaps it is both. When individual believers can be brought into the Christian Church and feel that the total function of the ministry is the responsibility of the pulpit, then the church is in trouble. Each member should feel that personal identification with the church is actually an induction into the personal ministry of Christ. A tragic truth is that this growing gap is usually overlooked.

Every member of the church, including the minister, is obligated to do basic New Testament evangelism. This is expressing through personal witness the "good news" of salvation which they have experienced by believing the Word of God. It is obvious from scripture that the minister who preaches, teaches and leads a congregation must also be individually involved in personal evangelism. He is not only the shepherd; he is also a sheep. He is not only a minister; he is first a layman. In the theocracy of grace, it is difficult to discern a scriptural difference between clergy and laity in the performance of personal ministry. The slight exception would be that the minister, in addition to his personal ministry, be responsible for corporate ministry and public preaching.

Quantitative growth is dependent basically upon the evangelistic outreach of the church and the mobilization of the church constituency to effect not only the maturing and equipping of the saints but also the ministry of the church. When individual believers are not equipped for Christian service, when they do not understand their role in the ministry, when their task is not clear, then they cannot participate in the ongoing program of the church. This leaves most of the public witness to the responsibility of the clergy and creates a considerable gap between the pulpit and the pew.

The New Testament never intended for this gap to exist. It can be traced back probably to the first structured church building where the minister stood up and the people sat down. Since that day, the congregation has been gathering, gawking and grudgingly giving of their time and means until many have developed a "cirrhosis of the giver." The minister is so actively involved in "his work" until the attitudes and potentials of the congregation are overlooked.

The work of ministering is clarified in Ephesians 4:7, 8. Each individual Christian has been chosen to exercise a specific responsibility. Some are in positions of leadership, yet each has a contribution that he alone can make to the church. Paul concludes his metaphor of a growing body with the thought that the body grows only as the individual members properly perform their functions. Human effort is an integral part of the divine plan.

In I Corinthians 12, four of the gifts of the Spirit are endowments bestowed upon individual Christians, which they are expected to exercise in the church. Here the gifts of the ascended Christ are the individual Christians who are personally endowed and then given by Christ to the church.

"Evangelists" and "teaching pastors" are required in each generation to perpetuate the church. The church can never dispense with men who preach the gospel and bring men to the saving knowledge of the truth, nor with men who can teach and guide in the way of truth those who have been evangelized and converted. The terms "pastors" (shepherds) and "teachers" denote one and the same class of men. They are the men who "tend the flock of God" and care for its well-being, showing other Christians by precept and example the path of Christian faith and life (I Peter 5:2; Acts 20:28). These are the same elsewhere called elders and bishops, one of whose qualifications is being "apt to teach" (I Timothy 3:2).

The purpose of these primary gifts to the church is "to equip the saints for work of service in building up of the body of Christ." This rendering of the verse is supported by the fact that there is a change of preposition in the verse from *pros* to *eis*; *pros* denoting the ultimate, *eis* the intermediate object. The gifts in verse 11 do not monopolize the church's ministry; their function rather is to help and direct the church so all menbers may perform their several ministries for the good of the whole.

"Perfecting" denotes equipment. As Paul uses the biological term "growth" in Ephesians 2:21 in a context where the figure of the body is used, the healthy growth of the believing community is the aim in view of all the ministries which the Lord has entrusted to His people. "Perfecting" means to mend, complete, fit out, to make one what he ought to be. The phrase may be taken to signify "the complete fitting out of the saints" for "ministering" or serving. All the arrangement is for service in the church and the "building up" of the body. The natural expression here would have been the "growth of the body of Christ," since the body is not an edifice, but an organism. The expressions "edify" and "build up" are favorite ones of Paul and his meaning is distinct and clear.

The list shows the function of "evangelists and teaching pastors." The work of the ministry is for all Christians, not just top level leadership. It is the task of the leadership to equip the saints so they can perform their "ministry." This unity in the faith is not so much the fact of "one faith" as the unity among believers which is produced by their common sharing of "the knowledge of the Son of God." Each individual Christian ought to grow into spiritual maturity, but maturity in the individual Christian is not enough: There must be spiritual maturity in the corporate action of the church. One indispensable prerequisite for such corporate maturity is spiritual unity.

A community of believers which manifests this "unity of faith" is a mature church in which the doctrine of the New Testament is not merely honored in word but exhibited in deed as a living reality. What is stated as the goal for the whole church can be sought and attained in particular local churches. He who ascended has given gifts in order to equip the people of God for their various forms of service so that the body of Christ may be built up to the point where all together they may reach the maturity of full-grown manhood.

The church can no longer tolerate Christians who are spiritual infants tossed about and carried this way and that with every wind of teaching. The church must not be misled by men's slight of hand and crafty practice of deceptive stratagems. Believers must live by the standard of truth and grow up in every way in love to match Him who is the Head—for it is from Christ that the whole body, adjusted and fitted together by every ligament with which it is supplied, by the harmonious functioning of each and every part, acquired the power to grow up as a perfect organism built up in love. Only harmonious spiritual functioning can narrow the gap and bring the pulpit and pew together as a strong link in the chain of evangelism.

11.

Weak Links
Endanger the Chain
of Evangelism

The link of understanding connecting the pulpit and
the pew is weakened by conflicting purposes. This en-
dangers the chain of evangelism necessary to reach the
community with the gospel. When Christians do not identify with the role of the minister, they do not involve
themselves in daily witness. Consequently, the truth
of the gospel remains within the four walls of the sanctuary
or concealed neatly in the mind of the congregants. This
isolation of truth segregates spiritual concern to the pulpit
and deprives the church of the vitality necessary for
growth.

Evangelism is not an end in itself.[14] A decision for
Christ is the doorway to discipleship and effective service.
Conversion is more than a one-time affair—it is the love
link to a life of commitment to Christ. Christ himself
said, "Come unto me . . . take my yoke upon you . . . learn
of me." Yet weak links endanger the chain of evangelism.
Why is it that converts do not become disciples and disciples fail to mature into apostles of the streets? Is it
that they do not learn how to live their faith? Is it that
they are afraid to venture into the world, or is it that

they have just never developed a New Testament capacity to love?

The Christian life is a life in which one learns to love. On one occasion a Jewish religious leader asked Jesus what was the greatest commandment (Mark 12:28-34). Jesus replied that the greatest commandment was to love God with all one's heart and to love one's neighbor as one's self. Love is the link in evangelism. Love is the bridge across the great fixed gulf that lies between the saint and sinner. God is love and those who are born of God receive His love. God's love is shed abroad in man's heart and it is through this love that the Spirit motivates men to become adequate in evangelism.

Love is the never failing source of strength. Some think God has reserved love to Himself as the only weapon to conquer rebellious man. The love of God that is shed abroad in the hearts of men by the power of the Spirit is the compelling force that moves men into a world to demonstrate God's love. Love wins, survives and conquers and is the penetrating force that pierces even the stony hearts of men.

The convert becomes a weak link in the chain of evangelism when he fails to develop the capacity to love. This comes because the convert fails to grow in grace and knowledge. A Christian is expected to grow in at least two spheres of life: in understanding and in holiness of life. When the Christian life is begun, the believer understands very little and has only a vague concept of God. He must increase in the knowledge of God and of his Lord and Savior (Colossians 1:10 and II Peter 3:18). This knowledge is partly intellectual and partly experiential. Some is imparted by dynamic and sincere preaching; other aspects of understanding and knowledge comes in the quietness of a private devotion through personal Bible reading or in practical experience as a Christian. To neglect to grow in love and Christian understanding is to court disaster in the Christian life.

The New Testament writers speak concerning the development of faith in God and love for others. Every con-

vert to Christ longs to become more conformed in his
character and behavior to the Son of God Himself. The
Christian life is a life of righteousness. The Holy Spirit
has been given to enable believers to obey God's commandments and do God's will. As the believer allows the
Spirit to continuously fill him with His power, the Spirit
will subdue evil desires and cause His fruit to appear
which is: love, joy, peace, longsuffering, gentleness, faith,
meekness, goodness and temperance.

It is difficult if not impossible for an unloved person
to love others. Part of the reason for a failure as a Christian to love others is that the believer himself does
not feel loved. When an individual understands that he
is loved, it is the most natural thing in the world for love
to be shared. Christians are promised God's love and can
expect God to daily issue this love freely to meet all of
man's "love needs" and enable him to give love to others.

What is love? Love is not romance or a warm feeling
one has for another person since Christ tells the believer to love even his enemies. He did not say romance
your enemies, the command is to love them. Then what
is love? I Corinthians 13, a most majestic piece of literature and intensely practical, is a guide to loving other
people. The first part of this chapter tells what makes
a man great. It simply says that the measure of a man
is how much he loves. It is as simple as that. If he loves,
his potential is great as a soul winner and he will be an
effective Christian. The second aspect of this chapter
gives an anatomy of love. Paul tells what love is and what
love is not. He says that love involves action. Love is
not just "feeling"; love is doing certain things and avoiding other things. Love becomes the guideline of the Christian's daily life. The latter part of this chapter makes
it clear that love is eternal and that it will never end.

Only when a man is convinced that God loves him to
the point of sacrificing His own Son can he accept eternal
life. Eternal life only has meaning when that love is shared
with others in this life. Love is an art and requires knowledge and effort. The majority of believers today are not

convinced that this is true and this is the major cause of weak links in the chain of evangelism.

The problem of love for most people is primarily that of being loved rather than that of loving. Instead of developing an individual capacity to love, they pursue efforts to make themselves lovable. They often follow the same paths that one would follow to be "successful." They seem to be more interested in popularity and sex appeal than in a true capacity to express love. The problem of love for others is one of an object and not the problem of action. They search for the right object to love rather than cultivating the proper attitude to love all of God's creations. These problems complicate the expression of love and the action necessary to cause men to want to learn about Christ and His way of life.

Love always finds a way. Yet the usual excuse for not sharing faith verbally with others is that "I cannot express myself." Could it be that the experience is not deep enough or that the relationship to Christ is not meaningful enough to create a desire to share and tell? Concern about what people think rather than concern for sharing the "good news" often is the problem. Perhaps it is fear that questions cannot be answered correctly, or simply that people are not interested. But people are interested in love.

Everyone enjoys "good news." Mankind longs for inner peace. Everyone wants a quiet heart and all are seeking love and happiness. It is obvious then that weak links endanger the chain of evangelism because many do not have a real faith to share and others do not know how to witness with love. The Apostle John made it clear that "perfect love casteth out fear." God's love can teach men how to truly love others. All that is required is an open and receptive heart.

Sure, opposition is to be expected from others, but love will find a way. Opposition is hard to take. Everyone dislikes controversy. Some are prone to alter ideas when others disagree or to retract unpopular statements but love perseveres and pursues the right course. Christians need other people. There is no doubt about this. Without other people, life would be dull and meaningless. It is this need for fellowship and the desire to share with others that motivates believers to witness. It is selfishness and indifference to personal needs and the needs of others that cause Christians to become weak links in the chain of evangelism.

People seek true friends because they want the privilege of being honest and the opportunity of being themselves. Could it be that Christians who fail to witness fail to seek new friends for Christ and the church? Perhaps they do not want to be honest or do not wish to be themselves. Could this be the reason for hypocrisy existing in the church today? When believers experience authentic Christian fellowship, they discover the freedom to "be themselves." They can be honest because they understand God's forgiveness. Pretense or hypocrisy is unnecessary.

True fellowship is characterized by an atmosphere of love and forgiveness. Men forgive because God forgives. Men forget because God does not remember their wrong doings. Could it be that weak Christians do not want to forgive or forget? Is that the reason some do not reach out into the community to bring their enemies or strangers into the church? Could this not be a reason for many weak links in the chain of evangelism?

Christian fellowship requires mutual love (John 15:12-17). Loving one another is the foundation of fellowship and without this mutual love there can be no fellowship. Love is necessary for fellowship because only when one is loved can he open himself to others. When hostility prevails, the guard goes up. This causes caution and questions, but love gives confidence and security.

Love and fellowship also require burden bearing and sharing of problems (Galatians 6:1). This is the acid test for Christians. Authentic love for others expresses itself through burden bearing. Their problems become part of our burden. To the Christian, a shared problem is one that is half way to being solved. Help, counsel, love and insight for the needs of others are vital to Christian fellowship and evangelism.

Love and fellowship require unity (Ephesians 4:1-6). Men who are born again share a common ground in Christ. A spiritual heritage binds them together regardless of other differences. Language, culture, speech, economic or social plane, the color of skin or political views, should make little difference. When these differences alienate men or cause men to question their witness, or going forth into the world, men become weak links in the chain of evangelism and the progress of the church is greatly endangered.

Weak links are caused in the chain of evangelism because of this wide gap between what Christians often profess and what they actually experience. There is a lack of power, a shuning of evangelistic responsibility because church members have nothing to give away. There is an absence of joy because there is little Christian experience. Since the Christian experience gave some so little satisfaction it must have been a very small experience. This obvious chasm between what is and what ought to be creates weak links in the chain of evangelism.

A Christian is never true to his conversion when he lives for himself. Each man is saved that he may serve Christ and because he is saved, he does serve the cause of right. The main responsibility is always outside the walls of the church in the unredeemed community. This is why God has placed a constraining love within the heart of each believer that compels him to witness and share his faith.

This gives the Christian movement its outgoing character so crucially important to its progress. If this reaching out is altered or rejected, then the program of evangelism dies. Actually, no one is really a Christian at all unless he is an evangelist or is making urgent preparations to become one. Those who think they can be Christians by staying out of trouble and being nice have missed the whole idea. The church today is not affecting the world because weak witnesses are weak links in the chain of evangelism.

12.

Cheap Grace
Produces
Poor Converts

Perhaps the most serious consequence of a weak pulpit is the preaching of cheap grace. This easy going, conciliatory approach to evangelism produces poor converts who can never stand alone, much less maintain a consistent Christian walk. This inadequate comprehension of conversion causes the church great difficulty in leading a new convert into an active life as a Christian disciple.

An adequate church is made up of responsible and thoroughly evangelized members. The involvement of this vital principle is essential to effective evangelism. Accepting Christ as Savior also means accepting Him as Lord. The "cost of discipleship," as Bonhoeffer calls it, stands out in the New Testament in sharp contrast to the easy "only believeism" of modern evangelism. Bonhoeffer said, "Cheap grace is the deadly enemy of the church." "Christianity without discipleship is always Christianity without Christ." [15] The first step in evangelism is not completed until the convert is made an active disciple of Christ.

During a prison riot one politician jokingly stated, "Well never have decent prisons as long as we keep sending criminals there." This goes along with a southern governor's explanation of his problems in rehabilitating prisoners. On national television, after a defense of the prison reform programs of his administration, he was asked the question, "Why are you not rehabilitating more criminals?" His simple answer was, "I can't do a better job until I get a better grade of convict." [16] This is exactly the problem of the church. The church cannot do a better job of winning the world until it gets better converts.

The quality of the convert is in direct relationship to the quality of the proclamation. When the minister preaches cheap grace and only believeism, men often accept Christ for the wrong reasons. Glamorous pulpit personalities produce converts with "preacher religion." When church buildings become monuments to personalities and synonymous with culture and social standing in the community, "church converts" are produced. Such converts represent intellectual knowledge with little or no personal experience. There may even be a verbalization of the doctrine but little if any internalizing of the truth. A young people's tract speaks to the issue: "If being born again didn't give you much satisfaction, try being born again." The same goes here. If the experience did not work, it's not the right experience.

There is more to accepting Christ than signing a card, being baptized, joining a church or shaking hands with the preacher. The cost of following Christ is measured in terms of total surrender to Christ as Lord and Master of life. True conversion affects the whole of life and living.

God will step into the life of any man who will walk the Calvary road, and that man will experience a conversion. This experience takes place when man is made aware of his own sinful, self-centered nature and confronts the Incarnate God at Calvary. Man's will is bowed and redirected toward God in total surrender and fusion with the will of God. His emotions are stirred by this tremendous experience. The Calvary encounter or conversion is completed when man, seeking to find realization and fulfillment of his essential nature, accepts forgiveness of sins and is restored to fellowship with God.

God calls men to absolute conformity to the image of Christ. Nothing less than this did God propose and with nothing less should the believer be content. God called man to fellowship with His Son on earth, both in His sufferings and His joys. The object of God's call is that man might be holy now and have full fellowship with Him. As man draws nearer to God the Father, he is conscious of the divine presence and companionship with the risen Lord. His countenance radiates the glow of God's glory. The believer's faith gives substance to the presence of Christ until the very words of his prayers, by faith, are as satisfying as if the Master's garment had been touched.

The general picture evoked by the Gospels is one of a strong movement stirred up by Jesus among the people. Crowds pressed around Him, listened eagerly to His words, and were amazed at the authority of His teachings. They sought His healing power and praised the miracles He performed. As a result of His ministry, many persons attached themselves to Jesus in varying degrees of conviction and loyalty. This frames the many individual scenes from the story of Jesus, but these followers do not constitute His disciples. To follow someone from place to place does not mean discipleship.[17]

A broad and a narrow use of the term is discernible in the Gospels and is seen to the best advantage in connection with the choice of the twelve disciples. This group of disciples, *par excellence*, was chosen from a larger company of disciples. By virtue of this selection the term disciple was narrowed to this group by traditional usage. During the ministry of Jesus, numerous others were designated as disciples. Those who followed Christ were commonly known as "His disciples," thus the contemporaneous description of the term has been preserved. Jesus had twelve disciples, seventy disciples, and a great multitude of disciples. There were active disciples and passive disciples, true disciples and false disciples.

The Gospels do not teach that salvation and discipleship are two distinct things, but that they are two parts of a single experience which involves one's relationship to Jesus Christ as Savior and Lord. It is clear that Jesus taught that when one is saved he becomes a disciple. The New Testament presents Jesus Christ as both Savior and Lord and requires that He be accepted and followed.

Jesus was extremely popular as long as He was healing the sick and feeding the multitudes, but when the people discovered the demands of His discipline, they wanted nothing more to do with Him. It seemed that Jesus was always whittling down the multitudes that followed Him. Those who were there for the "loaves and fishes" soon departed. The demands of discipleship were too difficult for them.

On one occasion Jesus even asked the disciples who remained, "Will ye also go away?" Realizing that salvation and discipleship were bound together they answered: "To whom shall we go? Thou hast the words of eternal life." Those who remained were willing to abide by the requirements of discipleship and be counted on to obey the commandment of Jesus.

The seriousness of the call is demonstrated by the earliest disciples. Their encounter with Jesus was a testimony to His absolute and direct authority. Jesus called them and expected them to obey, which resulted in salvation and discipleship. "Follow me" simply meant that they were to forsake all and to follow in the footsteps of Jesus; not that there was glory in following, but that the individual may serve as a disciple. The old things, with their relative security, forsaken for that which seems to be absolute insecurity. However, complete abandonment to Christ becomes security and safety as one walks in the fellowship with Jesus. Only those truly committed to Christian discipleship are worthy of being called converts. Complete surrender alone is adequate preparation to follow Christ.

When showmanship or cheap psychology is used to attract converts to follow a preacher or a "doctrine" the whole cause of Christianity is weakened. Faith comes by hearing the Word from a preacher, teacher or friend. Only the Word can adequately change the lives of men and make them true followers of Christ. Anything less or more weakens the quality of the convert and limits his ability to become a consistent Christian who daily practices discipleship.

13.

Converts
Do Not Become
Disciples

The business of making disciples throughout the world is the primary work of the church. However, the process of making disciples requires that individual converts be nurtured into disciples and equipped as apostles to go forth with the message to everyone they meet.

Efforts are made to reach the masses with the basic gospel, but very little is done to make these converts into adequate disciples of Christ. The church has a right to expect a rapid growth in depth and power towards Christ, fellow Christians and even the world, as an immediate result of the transforming power of conversion. There is a discrepancy in the depth of the work compared with the breadth. The preaching of the gospel that brings revival proclaims that Christ died for sins. But salvation can never be a passive experience. People cannot accept Christ intellectually and then play the role of a Christian without being involved intimately and individually in the daily work of Christ in the world.

Having the mind of Christ would certainly send each

man into the work-a-day world as a living witness to
His saving grace. This is the reason the Apostle Paul
labored night and day with tears to present the whole
gospel balanced and withheld nothing that would serve
to equip his converts for proclaiming the good news
(Acts 20:27-31). Evidently Paul knew of the problems
brought about by a partial or one-sided presentation of
God's plan of salvation. God not only offered salvation;
He made opportunity for service.

The church has failed to lift up Jesus Christ as the real
Savior and Lord of men's lives. The claims of discipleship
have not been placed before the people who profess Christ.
The church secured only decisions and stopped short
of "making disciples." Christian discipleship is still
possible and Jesus Christ still demands it. The call
"Follow Me" was made to each man who lives. Christ demands decision. He demands discipleship. The choice is
clear: discipleship for converts or disaster for the church
and the expansion of Christianity.

The new discipline taught and lived by Jesus Christ,
demands discipleship and produces two practical problems. First, one must apply the new discipline to his life;
second, he should find the power to accept and to put the
demands into action. These are man's most urgent and
most practical problems. Discipleship is demanded by
Jesus Christ, and it requires a personal decision to follow
Him.

When Christ calls a man to follow Him, He expects the
person to apply the new discipline to his life. Jesus Christ
is the same and the requirements of discipleship have
not changed. Christ Himself furnishes the strength to
follow. He manifested amazing confidence in average
men and committed into their hands the work of the
kingdom. Jesus had unwavering confidence in the men
who accepted His discipline. He was certain that the
growing power of His teaching on their lives and deeds
would be sufficient to produce disciples of distinction
for the kingdom.

The objective of Christ's Commission is the making

of disciples. Throughout the history of man, God has been in the process of teaching men, of making disciples and of creating His glorious likeness within them. It is through these means that He is preparing them for a new world order designated as His kingdom. God expects the followers of Christ to be busy in the world, making disciples by precept and practice.

The conditions of discipleship must never be understood as a moral code that Jesus demanded from only a few. All who would follow Christ and be His disciples must meet the same conditions. There can be no exceptions.[18]

Men did not follow Jesus blindly. He told them what it would cost to be His disciple. Jesus invited men to come and to take up His yoke as a mark of discipleship. Those who desired to be disciples must count the cost. It was necessary to take these steps: forsake all, deny self, take up the cross, and follow Christ.

Jesus declared that those who would not forsake everything could not be His disciples. All conflicting loyalties must be put aside. He said exactly the same things about salvation and discipleship. The rich young ruler was told "... sell all ... come ... follow me." Nothing less than complete dedication was sufficient. When Jesus insisted that a man must "hate" his family, friends and possessions, He did not mean that men should despise these things (Luke 14:26; Matthew 10:36-39). Jesus wanted His followers to have the love of a family, share the joy of friendship, and possess sufficient earthly goods to insure a happy life, but He did not want these things to hinder discipleship.

Christ demanded priority. Jesus was comparing human love to the new spiritual love the disciple would have for the heavenly Father. Compared to the human emotion and physical attachment the spiritual love of the disciple was to be so great that all else seemed as hate. However, there are cases in which men must literally forsake all earthly attachments to assure that proper attachment to Christ, but in such the disciple is promised "an hundredfold" reward in this life, and in the world to come he is promised eternal life (Matthew 19:29).

Denying self is accepting Jesus Christ as Lord. This is a vital part of discipleship. Man must be "delivered from the body of this death." Selfish ambitions have no place in discipleship. The capital "I" in SIN is the source of most human difficulties. S. D. Gordon aptly expressed the idea when he said, "In every redeemed heart there is a throne and a cross. If self is on your throne, Jesus is on the cross. . . . If self is your king, if self is on your throne, Jesus is on the cross. . . . Let self be on the cross and Jesus on the throne." Self must be crucified; Christ must rule and reign.

The disciple must be identified with Christ, and the cross is that identification. There is only one cross, the cross of Jesus Christ. This is the "yoke" of which Jesus spoke, the symbol of death. The believer must be "crucified with Christ" to become His disciple. Christians should not sing, "Jesus, I my cross have taken. . . ." In reality it is, "Jesus, I Thy cross have taken, all to leave and follow Thee." Taking up the cross is the disciple's way of saying "yes" to Christ and "no" to self. This is the only way to be free from self. Until an individual is willing to take up the cross and to follow Jesus, he is not worthy to be a disciple.

Obeying the call means following Jesus Christ. This must be the innermost longing of the soul. Following Christ includes a desire to know Him in the power of His resurrection and in the fellowship of His sufferings. Following Christ causes the believer to be made conformable unto His death and makes him willing to take up His cross. Any who will not follow Christ and will not meet these conditions has no right to claim to be His disciple. Those who will not be a disciple have no reason to claim to be a Christian. The Christian must first be a disciple of Jesus Christ.

What does it mean to be a Christian? The disciples were first called Christians at Antioch. They were first of all disciples of Christ and, because of their association with Him and His way of life, they became known as Christians. The term identified their relationship with Christ. It is tragic that many desire to be Christians but are not willing to pay the price of discipleship. These would-be disciples desire to reduce discipleship to the level of their lives and to stipulate their own terms for salvation.

There are three such would-be disciples spoken of in Luke's Gospel (9:57-62) that adequately present the problems of converts who do not become disciples. The first would follow Jesus without waiting to be called and Jesus warns him that he does not understand the meaning of discipleship. The disciple is called to a life of self-sacrifice and service. Without the call of Christ, the individual would not be able to pay the price.

The second would-be disciple is called by Jesus to follow Him, but he wanted to bury his father first! At the critical moment when Jesus calls a man to follow Him, nothing—not even law itself—must act as a barrier to discipleship. The ones called must accept the absolute authority of Jesus and must follow Him without hesitation.

The third would-be disciple was similar to the first who offered to follow Jesus on his own initiative, but this one was bold enough to stipulate his terms. He was not willing to give Jesus priority. He placed a barrier between Christ and himself by wanting to go first and to bid farewell to his family and friends. This was a normal thing to do, but Christ had called him and He demanded first place in that life. He wanted to follow, but he felt obligated to insist on his own terms. Discipleship to him was something that he could choose for himself at his time and at his place and at his price.

This could never be Christian discipleship. These three would-be disciples illustrate some of the basic problems of discipleship: hearing the call, forsaking all, denying self, counting the cost, and following Christ. These difficulties, compounded many times in many places, have vitiated the victory strategy initiated by Christ through a basic conversion experience. The church cannot be triumphant on earth until Christ reigns in the hearts and lives of those who profess to follow Him. This is not a new problem. Old problems need old solutions. No program of renewal or expansion can be adequate alone. The simple solution to spiritual growth has always been the touch of the hand of God.

14.

Disciples
Do Not Become
Apostles

The power of the indwelling Holy Spirit makes Christian disciples into fervent apostles of Jesus.[19] What is so strange about being an apostle? Jesus Christ frequently described Himself as "one sent out" from the Father into the world to bear witness to the truth and to bring men to God through the sacrifice of Himself. What is more, the church appears in the New Testament as "Christ's living body of called out ones." It existed, not out of the world but in the world, as a witnessing community, reaching out in love to every man and place. Early believers are pictured as being conscious of an all-controlling life purpose which they attributed to God. They were men with a mission, "sent out ones," called out of the world to be sent back into the world.

The outgoing character of the New Testament Church is often overlooked. The coming in has been emphasized at the expense of the going out. It must be remembered that the coming together of the saints was so that they could be equipped to return into the world to be effective witnesses. Christ called to Him twelve and began to send them out (Mark 6:7). He sent the seventy "on ahead of Him" (Luke 10:1). Those who follow Christ as His disciples must also be sent forth as His apostles.

This transformation is vital to the work of the church. Individual believers assemble in the House of Prayer for the worship of God and the ministry of the Word and are transformed into disciples and apostles of the streets. It is the leadership of God-called men and the power of the Holy Spirit that transforms individual disciples into living apostles that are in service for Christ and the community.

Take a look at Luke's picture of the early church in Acts. These first-century Christians were possessed of an astonishing enthusiasm to witness to their faith in word and deed. It is precisely this spirit that accounted for the amazing spread of Christianity in those early days. These believers were compelled by a sense of mission stronger than death. Persecution merely fanned the flame. Wherever they went, they lived, they spoke the Word.

This may be a desperate day in human history, but what a great day for faith that "works by love"! Never since the first days of the church has the need, the opportunity for Christian witness been greater—witness that speaks the whole truth of God to the whole life of man because the Christian life and the church share a common goal: they exist for witness.

Christ's commission provided ample authority but lacked adequate motivation. The commission to disciple the nations necessitated Pentecost. Disciples were to wait in Jerusalem for an endument with power. They had the desire to go. They had a program and a reason for going. But God's work can never be done by human effort alone. Christ's disciples needed the inner motivation and leadership of the Holy Spirit to adequately fulfill the task of reaching their world for Christ. The commission is never clear unless it can be seen in the context of the inner "go ye" and enablement provided by the Holy Spirit at Pentecost. When the New Testament Church met opposition they turned to the Spirit for assistance (Acts 4:29-33). The phenomenal success of Paul's ministry can be attributed to the unique dynamic of the Spirit. This essential element of the Spirit made the early church triumphant. It is also indispensable in these "last days."

The Spirit in man is the answer to mediocrity. Experiencing the power of the Holy Spirit in the full personal equation can transform any man into an instrument of God. A perpetual rediscovery of Pentecost experientially is the key to power in evangelism and an adequate Christian witness.[20]

True apostleship comes as a result of an outpouring of the Holy Spirit on willing and submissive people. Active apostleship is the church coming alive to participate in evangelism. However, before evangelism takes place there must be an awakening. This awakening among the community or the mass population is a result of spiritual renewal within the church.

A spiritual awakening produces an awareness of "soul" and a desire for personal changes and for the altering of society. This is often expressed in folk movements where people demonstrate their desire for change. The expression of such movements are personal but the individuals are bound together by common desires and goals. They need each other.

A church committed to telling the "good news" must take advantage of the awakening by implementing avenues of enlistment and evangelism. Often whole groups are won when opinion leaders are converted. Sometimes, however, the church is guilty of using resources and leadership to perpetuate a spiritual atmosphere without implementing evangelism of the unconverted masses outside the church. To evangelize is to present Jesus Christ in the power of the Spirit that men may come to put their trust in Him as Savior and serve Him as Lord in the vocations of the common life. To proclaim the gospel is not enough. Proclamation must have the power of the Holy Spirit. The Spirit wants to use people. Individuals may personally prepare for a ministry of apostleship through submission and faith. God sends spiritual power to enable His followers to evangelize the lost.

Fear of defeat is the single greatest enemy of evangelism (Matthew 25:15). The parable of the talented servant whose phobia caused him to default, gave fear as his defense. He said, "I was afraid." He was called an unprofitable servant. Faith can conquer fear, because faith brings out hidden strength. Believers are strong. Timid or fearful soldiers are of little value in the Lord's army. The interval between Christ's ascent and His return must be used by intrepid disciples to evangelize the world. Christ initiated His program for world evangelism by hand-picking the twelve. The New Testament Church had a Spirit-picked but predominantly masculine leadership. This scriptural precedent declares that men are God's method and message.

The female role was a supporting role. Deborah, the only women ever to judge Israel, recruited Barak to champion the cause (Judges 4:4-9). She declared her willingness to go with him into battle, not instead of or ahead of him. Today, however, men often let women take the lead and by default loose the leadership and blessing of directing God's work. Ezekiel declared that God "sought for a man among them, that should make up the hedge, and stand in the gap. . . ." God looks for men. God wants twentieth-century apostles to go with His message of saving grace! Praying mothers, faithful wives or the Women's Missionary Society can never do the job alone. Men must be both willing and desirous of becoming "apostles of the streets."

Straight, 'Stablished and Stuck

(Organization-Centered Problems)

Churchmen often consider doctrinal orthodoxy sufficient to guarantee growth and progress for the church. This attitude obstructs the inherent factors of growth and causes churchmen to be content with mediocrity. The willingness to settle for something less than the best causes the church to suffer from spiritual disease and to become strangulated in vital areas of growth and progress. The willingness to settle for mediocre operations also brings about a lack of global perspective and produces a neglect of planting new churches.

15. Doctrinal Orthodoxy Is Considered Sufficient
16. Inherent Growth Factors Are Obstructed
17. Churchmen Are Content with Mediocrity
18. Church Suffers from Spiritual Disease
19. Church Is Strangulated in Vital Areas
20. Global Perspective and Concern Are Missing
21. Church Planting Is Neglected

15.

Doctrinal Orthodoxy
Is
Considered Sufficient

Because the church is right in doctrine, some believe it has the might to accomplish all desired ends. Adequacy in meeting the needs of contemporary society is not necessarily subsequent to the acceptance of basic and true doctrine. Right is might only when doctrine is the foundation of duty. It is true that faith determines practice but all that is classified as doctrine by the church is not brought into practical application of life. In fact, when the theology of the church is not put into practice, for all practical purposes the church has no doctrine at all.[21]

Doctrine is the raw material of the Word which councils the church in the formulation of theological truth. The implication of doctrine in the Old Testament was to receive or to hear. In the New Testament, doctrine suggests the act of teaching (communicating) the content of the faith. With this in mind, there can be no doctrine unless there is communication of the content of the Word. Learning cannot take place unless there is teaching.

Doctrine and spiritual life ought to be complimentary. "Sound doctrine" affirms that true doctrine is life giving (I Timothy 1:10; Titus 2:1). The letter alone killeth, but the Spirit gives life to the letter. Giving life to the letter is a real problem of the contemporary church. The doctrine, the teaching, even the authoritative ecclesiastical affirmation is weakened by the lack of spiritual life and understanding.

Obviously orthodoxy alone is not sufficient. To have a right opinion about the New Testament or to possess no taint of heresy is not sufficient to guarantee that the world will beat a path to the door of the church. Certain statements of doctrine, accurately embodied reveals the truth content of Christianity and are in their own nature, normative in the church universal. Yet the church universally does not grow in proportion to population.

No churchman worth his salt will deny that rooted in the New Testament is an insistence that the gospel has specific factual and theological content (I Corinthians 15:1-11; Galatians 6:9). Most churchmen will agree that there is no fellowship existing between those who accept the apostolic standard and those who deny it. Yet, those who accept in good faith, this standard, seem to be preoccupied with preservation of Christianity rather than the expansion of the Christian faith. There is confusion over the experiential aspects of doctrine and practice.

The church must live the message it preaches. Christians must experience and live the New Testament doctrine to be adequate advocates of the Christian faith. It is tragic for churchmen to believe that embracing certain cardinal truths or affirming certain principles of doctrine is sufficient to guarantee the growth of the church.

Obviously, the church believes the Bible. Many man hours and millions of dollars through the years have gone into churches and seminaries to perpetuate these doctrinal principles. Yet there is room in the churches for the lost and dying world and room in the hearts of Christians for tender love and compassion for their fellowman. Much of the money and a great deal of the time seems to have been wasted on preservation of doctrine. Very little of the doctrinal truth implanted in the head has filtered through to the heart and influenced the daily lives of church members.

To be sufficient is to be enough to meet the needs and provide a solution for a proposed end. The goal and objective of the church is to bring all men to a saving knowledge of Christ. Churchmen must admit that possessing a doctrinal statement has not been sufficient to bring men to this desired end.

To produce an adequacy, the church must experience the doctrine it believes and practice it daily in life. True, there ought to be an intellectual apprehension of truth, but there must be more. There must be a practical application of what one believes. The tragedy of weak and weary witnesses, the disgrace of dying or dead churches, points directly to the fact that there is little personal experience or application of the cardinal and fundamental truths proclaimed by the church for generations.

Churchmen must seek ways of getting the doctrine out of the book and into the hearts of the people. The church must find a vehicle to carry the men who have the message into the world. Doctrine is a firm foundation upon which to stand, but experience is necessary to storm the ramparts and reach to the uttermost parts of the earth with the transforming message of Christ. The power of spiritual experience can be the means of transforming the letter of doctrine into the life of the church. Personal spiritual involvement alone can assure an adequate witness and continued renewal!

Generally, "slow growth indicates that something is wrong with the quality of life in the church." [22] Either the church lacks the urge to make disciples or does not have the faith and victory necessary to translate evangelistic urge into an effective endeavor. It is reasonable to expect that a church in which the Holy Spirit is at work will experience rapid growth as did the New Testament Church. There is abundant evidence around the world in Brazil, in Chile, in Indonesia and in Latin America that rapid growth continues to be the norm for New Testament congregations.

Church growth around the world is preceded by the unusual and dynamic impact of the gospel in the lives of people. At conversion and as the convert grows in grace and knowledge, the Holy Spirit teaches and guides into all truth. Consequently, a powerful and adequate personal witness exists as a part of the expansion of the church. Only later, as things slow down does the church, by attempting to inculcate a stereotyped doctrinal statement, complicate the understanding of dogma. Thus, the spontaneous application of truth to life is limited by an effort to obtain a doctrinal frame of reference. This further complicates and slows the growth and progress of the church.

The New Testament Church trained by the Lord and directed by the Spirit grew rapidly. In the case of New Testament discipleship, thousands accepted Christ and were received into the church simply by believing the Word, repenting of their sins and declaring their faith. The New Testament also makes it clear that once converts were initiated into the church they immediately "devoted themselves to the Apostles teachings and fellowship, to breaking of bread and to prayers." The Lord added to their numbers, day by day, those who were being saved. Day by day they attended the Temple together, breaking bread in the homes and partaking of food with glad and generous hearts and having favor with all the people. The church continued to grow rapidly.[23]

Many walls of isolation were broken down not by declaring doctrinal distinctiveness, but through the spontaneous witness of believers. New Testament witness became a force stronger than the differences which had kept men apart. A new dynamic came into play and brought men together in a comprehensive and enriching fellowship. The New Testament Church saw timid Galilean fishermen transformed under the impact of the resurrection and Pentecost, become men of fearless courage. The common people continued to respond with repentance and faith. Priests, captains in the Temple and other leaders eagerly turned to the gospel. There was opposition, but unnatural alliance could not stop the growth of a church that had been thrust into the world with the saving message. When doctrine proceeds beyond the head and is experienced in the heart, the New Testament dynamic works. Individuals believe and witness. The church grows and the truth prevails.[24]

16.

Inherent Growth Factors Are Obstructed

God established dynamic organization as an essential part of the church. The organization was to be a physical force producing action. The administration and functional structure was to bring the church into a coherent unity or functioning whole. Systematic planning, united effort and interdependent parts were all inherent in the arrangement of church organization. It is the frustration of these factors of organization that obstructs the progress of the church.[25]

Scripture does not present a detailed organizational plan for the church, but organization is a mark of the church. It is obvious that haphazardous or inefficient operation is not in keeping with the true character of the church. God expects His church to be both adequate and effective. Yet by ignoring essential aspects of organization, churchmen block the path to progress.

Systematic long-ranged planning is a vital function of organization. Only when churchmen consider the anticipatory aspects of growth and plan accordingly can progress be assured. One distinguishing feature characterizing normal developmental growth is its purposiveness and anticipation of future needs, not only for the individual but for the group. Detailed planning that denotes clear understanding of the growth process is a prerequisite to growth. When planning becomes limited enough to cut off from view the long-ranged objective, churchmen have drastically impeded progress.

Enlistment of new leadership is a vital function of organization and a key to growth. It is the responsibility of each person to reproduce himself, the normal saturation point being perhaps ten. Workers must feel a responsibility for enlisting and training replacements and additions to the staff. This is the only way the process of growth can continue. In spite of this fact, many churchmen seem more concerned with self-perpetuation and longevity than the involvement of new and creative talent. This hinders the necessary united effort of the congregation because a few individuals attempt to do all the work.

Cooperation and interdependency are necessary in all areas of church operation. A failure to plan for total participation builds obstacles in the way of fellowship and complicates any united effort. This breeds unnecessary competition and personal strife among the staff and frustrates the whole function of organization. Interdependency and unified support for the whole program are indispensable to church growth.

The dynamic aspects of organization includes several phases of growth and stages of development. A failure to understand these phases locks the thinking of churchmen into fixed attitudes that handicap the advance of the church. All phases of growth are temporary. This fact must be considered to understand the nature of growth are temporary. This fact must be considered to understand the nature of growth and to avoid obstructions to progress.

Although church organization is somewhat distinctive, church growth is not unique; it follows the pattern of nature. Early rapid growth gives way to healthy development through a constructive coordination of differing facets into a complete unit. Growth is not confined to the early stage; it continues as long as there is vitality. Life is growth and growth is change. Age retards the process but growth and change continue until death. Within this continuity there are many metamorphasis-like critical periods of discontinued growth. One thing is certain: the process of growth is dynamic.

Success tends to develop the seeds of failure. Consequently, growth develops a condition which may retard the process in accordance with the law of diminishing returns. The perpetual renewal of the whole structure is imperative to continued growth but the tendency is for this renewal to be at an ever decreasing rate. This is caused by a deterioration and hardening of the vital structures of growth. This loss of elasticity is reflected by a slowing down of the growth process with consequent increasing frequency of decay in various functions and facilities of the organization.

A closer look at the three main phases of the normal growth pattern makes the dynamic growth process of the church easier to understand. There are many interrelated categories of growth; however, church growth fits best in the growth pattern of multicellular organisms. This is growth by unit enlargement and unit division. The phenomenon is very complex but if follows a definite plan.

The pattern of development is almost identical to the S-curve of growth in plant and animal life. The shape of the normal growth curve reveals a similarity between growth curves of units and the whole. This is significant for church growth. The growth curve of the New Testament Church, modern denominations and local churches, follow a similar curve. This growth curve has two opposing forces: a self-accelerating slope and a self-inhibiting slope. A constant growth rate is common until the "frontierland" is used. Then following the use of all easily accessible areas, the growth-retarding factors eventuates the declining slope.

The initial growth of a church follows a simple logarithmic relationship. But as the "carrying capacity" of the social "habitat" is approached at the crisis point (X), the rate of growth decreases and may lead to a population of a fixed size (III or Y). If the social "habitat" is destroyed, changed or drastically altered, the population decreases in proportion to the decrease in the carrying capacity. On the other hand, if the population can alter its structure to meet the needs of a changing "habitat" it may stabilize and become fixed in size but be considerably smaller than its normal potential (Y or Z). (See Figure 1.)

For example: Pentecostals. The growing edge of the church in many parts of the world seems to have enlarged its "habitat." Its base of support has broadened from the "mountain folk" and the common man to include almost every segment of society. The Southern Baptists have also been most successful in broadening their "habitat" and enlarging their potential. Their heart-warming and often informal approach has strong appeal around the world. In most cases, they have not permitted the "gap" to develop between the pulpit and the pew. Their lines of communication remain open to the public. This is most likely the reason the Southern Baptists are the growing edge of the Baptist movement.

The S-curve of growth has three phases: a period called the lag phase (I) when preparation is being made for growth. The period of actual growth is called exponential or logarithmic phase (II). This period of rapid growth climaxes in maximum efficiency and usually gives way to a health development through a constructive coordination of differing facets of the population into a uniform whole. At this point in development a stationary phase (III) usually develops because of the effort of the organism or movement to survive. When the crisis is not met, the energies and resources normally used for outreach and expansion are rechanneled into the development of institutions designed to maintain the *status quo:* thus, the leveling off period is entered, when growth ceases and the size stabilizes. This is usually called the stationary phase and is the most critical. (See Figure 1.)

Figure 1. Diagram of the normal growth curve of populations. 1-5 same as Figure 1. I—lag phase, II—logarithmic phase, III—stationary phase. X—point of crisis. Y—decreased population. Z—fixed size below potential.

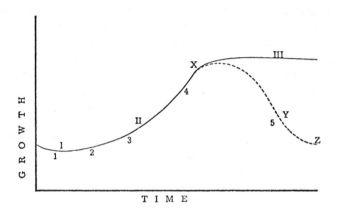

It is at the beginning of the stationary phase that the organization loses its flexibility and operations settle down to routine and reactionary activities. Leaders concentrate on programs, projects and reports that reflect their personalities and simulate progress. As the organization tightens a grip on the powers that be to perpetuate the *status quo*, the church begins to die. Leaders may project a saintly image and reports show active participation, but the progress is more material than it is spiritual.

Leadership must be aware that statistics alone cannot measure the vitality of religious experience. It is the effect the church has on society—the number of converts to the Christian faith, the number of believers who live their faith—and this must be considered in relationship to the size of the church. The essence of the church, influences the practical manifestation of the church. Care must be taken not to confuse this manifestation with the essence. The essential nature of the church is the possession and proclamation of the gospel. The gospel, therefore, is a common necessity and there is no way to outgrow the need for proclaiming the gospel.

A systematic and personalized involvement is necessary to continued growth. The language of words must be translated into a language of relationship. Even spasmodic ventures in people-to-people efforts have proved to be a tremendous growth factor. The active participation of laymen in a structured program of personalized outreach furnishes a church with a new fervor for New Testament evangelism, and an important factor becomes clear: God uses men to carry His message to the lost. A positive and progressive attitude is needed to see the magnitude of this opportunity. By ignoring this irreplaceable factor in church growth, churchmen impede the growth of the church.

A growing knowledge of the outreach potential demands an expanding structure and facilities for growth. Ignoring these factors confines the process of growth and development to periodic personnel changes and a turnover of adherents; thus, maintaining the *status quo* becomes the norm. Consequently, many churchmen are content with mediocrity and settle for gradualism in growth.

17.

Churchmen
Are Content
with Mediocrity

"The ability to look great opportunity for church growth squarely in the face and not see it is common." Basic thought structures prevent recognition of the significance of the opportunities for church growth. Many churchmen seem to be content with mediocrity of operation and gradualism of growth.[26]

Exploratory aspects of outreach blocks clear thinking. The policy of thrusting men into areas they do not understand to work with people whose culture or sub-culture is vastly different causes many problems. The church should take knowledge that Paul's contemporaries of the first century knew from childhood the language and culture" of those to whom they carried the gospel.[27]

An exploratory attitude brings about slow and small growth of the church. Converts are won with great difficulty. Many think it is self-evident that church growth comes very slowly. To these, evangelism is gradually presenting the gospel, sowing in hope and slowly penetrating an alien society. The New Testament atmosphere was different—it was militant and aggressive.

"Slow growth has developed a theology and organization to fit it." The essential duty of the Christian has become to witness, whether the hearers believe or not is of little concern; it is witnessing for witness sake. Scriptures are often used to support such action, but they do not ring clear as the New Testament pattern or agree with the consensus of Spirit-filled believers. It is contrary to a basic theology of harvest. Slogans are often developed to justify this approach: "One soul is worth the whole world." "God's way is a slow but sure way." [28]

When growth comes and then stops, the logical and accepted explanation is that "a period of consolidation must follow a period of growth." Sometimes this is "the rationalization of an unnecessary condition." Stop and go growth is often the result of limited planning and a low level of financial support. Arrested growth could usually be cured with a New Testament program of stewardship.[29]

Sometimes the acceptance of slow church growth is doubtlessly the will of God. This fact has probably kept many churches going in critical years of hardship. Thus, small churches became rooted, local leadership developed, and a foundation for the real penetration of society was laid. However, there comes a time to act; a time to launch a real thrust into the world. Tragically, the vision of many churchmen is limited by this point of view even though conditions have drastically changed.

The church must never despise the day of small things, but the glorification of smallness or slowness is tragic. Deep-seated convictions that church growth comes slowly must be changed. The material resources and trained leadership must now be deployed with a New Testament concept of total outreach.

A basic cause of retardation in church growth is communicating the faith only to those who are connected in some way with the church. This is usually done because of opposition from the outside. Christians become weary of persecution and desire to be free from the conflict necessary in public witness. Consequently, the church settles for mediocrity in program and gradualism in progress.

Whenever the church fails to witness adequately for Christ, growth is retarded. Loss of vitality within the congregation means that there can be no effective communication to the children of members or no successful dealing with those on the outside of the fellowship. To fail in the home or community is to retard the work of God and to hinder the growth of the church.[30]

Retardation not only affects individuals, it affects the whole church. God is not satisfied with minimal or moderate growth. Churchmen should repent rather than justify themselves. Retardation usually comes because there are spiritual needs in the lives of the membership that are not met. Therefore, the lack of spiritual vitality in the theology and practical workings of the church are basic causes for the lack of church growth.

Not only must the individual be spiritually fed to be an effective Christian, he must regularly communicate the "good news" about Christ to others. This is essential to the spiritual well-being of any believer. The lack of spiritual life usually breeds complacency. Indifference and complacency are the chief reasons for mediocrity and retarded growth.

Divided opinions and other devisive elements within the church also cause retarded growth. Any new barrier to Christian fellowship or opposition to basic communication becomes a major source of retardation. The tragedies of isolation and misdirection must be averted by the church if fellowship is to be vital and growing.

Church growth is much like the development of a child. "Adequate nutrition, a maturing social awareness, and intelligence are desirable elements in development; but were a child's weight to remain" the same for an extended period of time, "the mother would rightly feel anxious no matter how socially mature the child was. The one criterion—increase of bodyweight—is not enough but to disregard weight as a chief criterion is fatal."[31]

Yet this is often done in churches—growth in mem-

bership is not regarded as a chief consideration in esti-
mating church health. Churchmen take disastrous comfort in cliches that "while the church is not growing,
of course, it is maturing—or developing in self-aware-
ness or deepening its spiritual life, or becoming more
indigenous." Where growth is possible and not occurring,
the thought that "all is well, for we are concentrating
on the spiritual" is an opiate inducing a false sense of
well-being. Obviously, the matter of lack of growth is
being completely ignored.[32]

Churchmen who become content with a moderate or
low-level of church operation are only half way up the
mountain of progress. The summit of spiritual success
can never be reached as long as men settle for anything
less than the best in church organization and operation.
The willingness to stop short of total penetration of
society robs the church of the spiritual health which
permits the automatic and natural aspects of growth
to occur within the church structure.

18.

Church Suffers from Spiritual Disease

Many maladies plague the church because of lethargic and indifferent congregations. Most of the diseases encroaching on the spiritual health of the church are caused by churchmen who do not practice preventive medicine. God has ordained a regular ministry of the Word which includes confession and communion. Yet the clergy fails to communicate the Word, challenge the congregation, produce adequate confession or involve individuals in regular communion. Most of the ills can be traced to these sins of omission.

A failure to communicate the Word is the basic difficulty. By dividing the problem it can be seen more clearly. One half of the problem is failure of the clergy to adequately minister. The other part is the problem of the laity who evade God and fail to hear the Word when it is preached. Consequently, the major spiritual disease of the church is malnutrition.[33]

There is a famine in the land. Not of bread but of the Word of God. Ministers preoccupy themselves with current events and sermons with social and political implications rather than concentrating on the basic principles of life as presented in the Scripture. The meaning of the message is lost in the oratory, just as the sermon in the song is often lost in the rhythm and the beat of the music. The sacred meaning of the scaraments is lost in a ritualistic and perfunctory observance. Somehow the meaning does not penetrate the liturgy. The basic famine is one of hearing the Word of God.

Modern man has developed a unique ability to tune God out of his conscious mind. Spiritual things are relegated to some ancient cultural influence that has little bearing upon the implications of daily living. Present day congregations have developed the unique ability to hear the sound without hearing the sermon. This is spoken of in Scripture as people having "ears to hear, and hear not."

A newspaper story concerning a multimillionaire recluse, said that he was suffering from malmutrition. A man with the means to acquire food of any quality and in any quantity from anywhere in the world suffering from malnutrition is almost unbelievable. Yet it is possible for men of wealth and ambition to be so busy doing a multiplicity of "important things" that they would neglect to eat the proper foods and actually suffer from malnutrition.

The problem in the church is not the availability of food or the ability to acquire it but the deliberate evading of the message. The way men turn God off, change channels and refuse to accept the nutritious elements of the Word of God, brings about the disease of malnutrition. The whole intent and purpose of the church is weakened by this malady.

Men usually fail to eat properly when they have no sense of purpose or objective in life. Perhaps this is the basic cause for men refusing to hear the Word of God. Somehow the church has developed an inadequate sense of purpose. Congregations do not understand the purpose of the physical building or the framework of the spiritual house. Therefore, it is not likely they will become lively stones in the spiritual building. They may develop an eager but fruitless search for substitutes and produce synthetic or artificial ways of measuring church-related and spiritual accomplishments. The true purpose of the church, that of nourishing and equipping the saints to become adequate in personal soul winning, is neglected. The criteria of personal evangelism is not used to judge the adequacy of the congregation, because the basic purpose of the congregation is not understood.

This "inadequacy of purpose instills no will to grow."[34] The congregation seems satisfied to maintain the status quo and keep up the facade or form of worship that satisfies the conscience. There is no evangelistic urge, no desire to reach out to the lost and no desire to grow. When the church does not understand its purpose, individuals cannot be meaningfully involved in Christian service. Consequently, the church continues to suffer from the complications brought about by malnutrition.

Individuals do not have the spiritual desire or willingness to cooperate with God's plan or the preacher's ministry in reaching men. As men become satisfied and indifferent, the next step in spiritual decay becomes easy. They resist any move of the Holy Spirit to revive or renew their spiritual commitment. God willingly involves Himself in the lives of men to bring about an awareness of spiritual needs. Yet, when men refuse to listen to the Word of God, have little or no purpose in life, or become indifferent to spiritual things, it is easy for them to resist the Holy Spirit.[35]

Men resist the moves of the Holy Spirit to involve them in spiritual things because they are not willing to fulfill personal obligations in Christian service. The Holy Spirit constantly prods men into an awareness of the shortness of time. Not only for their personal benefit but so they can see how urgent it is that they individually be involved in the work of the church.

Perhaps the Pentecostals have the answer in their emphasis upon participation in congregational singing and concert prayer. The enthusiasm and involvement of this approach seems to say that each person is singing for his personal benefit alone. The melody of his heart is a pleasing response to his desire for worship. In concert prayer, each man seems to pray as if he were at home alone with the full realization that he is praying directly to God and not to be heard of others. Somehow this sparks a personal response between the worshiper and God that structures a frame of reference sufficient to guide his individual action throughout the week.

What the church often calls group action or corporate worship should be considered as personal training to perform as individuals in the work-a-day world. The goal of the church is not the gathering of the congregation but the precipitation of simultaneous individual Christian action within the community. Everyone, everywhere acting responsibly as Christians every day: this is evangelism. Simultaneous Christian action is the only work that can change the world. When every Christian begins to act individually and responsibly, things will improve.

Human frailness and spiritual weakness complicate the ongoing program of the church. The Holy Spirit is constantly in the world seeking men for kingdom work. Spirit-picked leaders within the church are active in presenting spiritual solutions to the problems of life but no one listens. No one hears the Word of God or feels the prodding of the Spirit. Consequently, the church drifts on in an indifferent, lethargic state suffering from spiritual disease that is a sickness unto death.

The only hope for new life within the church, the only salvation and spiritual renewal available is in the mercy and grace of God. Only the healing touch of the Master's hand can heal the fever of prejudice, break down the walls of sin that separate men and purge the sin of the heart and replace it with love. Only a divinely motivated operation of the Spirit can make the drastic alterations necessary to bring about the spiritual renewal within the church. The earthly Body of Christ suffers from spiritual disease and needs the healing touch of God. The medicine of men may delay the actual demise of the local congregation but only the touch of God can give it sufficient life to be adequate for this age.

19.

Church
Is Strangulated
In Vital Areas

Spiritual disease often precipitates the strangulization of vital areas within the church structure.[36] The principal weakness of a sick church manifests itself first in its leadership. As a leader is, so are the people. A basic quality of a good leader is the ability to persuade others to work together under his direction and as a team to accomplish certain designated objectives. When a leader loses this gift, his reputation vanishes and men no longer follow his direction.

The lack of spiritual fervor within the congregation breaks down the ability for a cooperative program and reflects directly upon leadership of the church. The greatest problem in leadership is the lack of stamina or staying power; consequently, there is little persistence in overcoming initial reverses and discouragement settles in very quickly to paralyze the ongoing program of the church.

This complicates the orderly administration and sound planning necessary to motivate a congregation toward renewal and growth. Leadership of the church often becomes a discouraging thing because of overwork and a multiplicity of involvement that could best be done by laymen. Churches are strangulated in the vital area of leadership because the congregations are not willing to emancipate the minister from mundane and routine duties so he may give himself to "prayer and study of the Word."

Most laymen are unwilling to provide an adequately paid church staff. Consequently, the church must depend on volunteer assistance. The majority of local leaders should be volunteers, but when there are too few volunteers and an insufficient staff, much of the work must be left undone or done by the minister.

Probably much of this problem exists because the obligations of leadership are not kept. There is little effort to organize team work or to identify with the goals of the congregation. In order to establish an adequate leadership image, the minister must have a clear sense of direction and firmness of decision. He should recognize and reward performance and make certain that everyone is treated justly. The team spirit should be maintained through out the whole program of the church.

Adequate leadership produces intelligent action not random activity. Leadership fails without a realistic and attainable goal or a plan that spells out, in an orderly fashion, how the church will arrive at its goal. Many churchmen do not do their homework or the advance ground work necessary to achieve action or to initiate the involvement of others. When church leaders do not begin with inner drive, continue by sorting out the vital from the trivial and climax in a concerted effort to reach the goals established by the congregations, church growth is stifled.

Leadership and fellowship are often confused. Church leaders are to ask the congregation to follow them as they follow the Lord, but too often the leadership follows the people rather than setting the pace and pattern for the congregation. Many churchmen today are similar to a personality in history who said: "There go the people, I am their leader, I must follow them." A leader must establish a lead not just be friendly. He must be an example. He must be able to make a decision and to lead the way. In this way he demonstrates his willingness to be involved in the work he asks others to do. There is no leadership without genuine "fellowship." When leadership fails to become involved in the work, the church becomes strangulated in the vital area of leadership. Men will not follow a weak leader.

The church is strangulated in the area of program because it is normally too complicated to be understood. It should be obvious to all men of leadership ability that no one can follow a program that is not clearly spelled out or easily understood. Inadequate programming brings about a constriction in vital functions of the church. It prevents individual initiative and complicates the circulation of vital information needed to advance the church.

An adequate leader develops a habit of a vigorous and positive approach to everything. He has a restless unhappiness with things as they are and an ever moving eye for possible improvements. An adequate leader programs to give individual freedom and initiative to subordinates and tailors or gears a program to the people involved. The more volunteer workers can participate in the decision process, the better they understand the program. Arbitrary and unilateral action must be avoided. Each member of the team should feel that he is an important part of the whole activity. Only then will the program work.

Perhaps the greatest problem precipitated by poor programming is the complications in eliminating wasted motion, unnecessary action or unproductive activity. Usually motion without real purpose or activity without real advancement, compresses and squeezes the very life out of a local congregation causing men to shrink from responsibility. Often objections to various aspects of local programming emerges and draws together isolated people who can rally around a point of opposition. Inadequate programming then is a place where the process of strangulation can restrict the whole progress of the church.

The problems of leadership and program can be solved locally by creative initiative and determination, but the church faces other problems that are not of a current nature. They are problems inherited from past leadership and programs that have outlived their usefulness. These problems concern the property and the social structure of the church and are the biggest areas of strangulation.

The church building shapes not only the size of the congregation but influences the program as well. The program is determined primarily by the community served by the church but must be altered to accommodate the limitations of the building complex itself. The church is for everyone, but there are very few conglomerate churches surviving to date. Churches normally structure themselves to reach a certain kind of people; people who enjoy certain types of preaching, singing or fellowship. Normally a local church ministers to a particular level of society. The church decides the people for whom it is responsible and constructs a building complex and structures a program and social concern in keeping with these goals. Instead of attempting to build one gigantic conglomerate congregation, it is usually better to plant several churches within a given area that could adequately minister to all the needs of the local constituency.

In planning a building complex, a church must determine its social structure. In doing this the church decides the kind of church it is to be, the kind of program it is to have, and the kind of people it is to reach. The basic problem with this situation is that as the needs of the congregation change and as the community itself changes, the church often is not willing to alter its structure to minister to the changing community. This causes a strangulation in these areas and severely handicaps the church in its ministry to the community.

Members regularly commute to a church building and return to a community that is virtually unchurched. It is obvious that the location of the property and the previously ordered social structure, strangulates the vital outreach of the church. It is easy to eliminate certain kinds of people or persons who live in certain sections of the city from any spiritual concern the congregation may have. It becomes easy to avoid anyone who is not similar in taste and social standing to those already making up the congregation. Consequently, the program of evangelism is stifled.

The large metropolitan churches that attempt to be conglomerate congregations are isolating themselves from many persons who could be won to Christ. Men normally will not cross cultural lines to become a Christian,[37] but will cross these barriers to obtain Christian fellowship. Most of these congregations are simply a gathering of various people who believe and want the same thing. This often conceals the real problem: the lack of adequate local churches in many parts of the city.

The conglomerate church can grow only to the degree that each small group has its needs cared for within the structure of the church. To survive, the metropolitan church must "find a way to surmount the mounting property barrier."[38] The price of land in the cities hinders growth. Beginning groups die because they cannot afford the property. For this reason, the small community church may be more adequate. The waves of migration into the cities points to the need to concentrate on "multiplying ethnic, class and language churches."[39]

Churches grow in proportion to the size of the group they are structured to reach. Normally, community churches do a better job of reaching and teaching the people. In a desire to be big, many metropolitan churches discard the quality of Christian influence in an effort to become a prestige congregation. Others who present an image of ministering to the whole city, are really a conglomerate only in the sense that the people are from various sources or areas of the city, but are not necessarily a different kind of people.

Obviously, changes need to be made in churches everywhere. These changes should include personnel, program, property and social structure. The courage to prune personnel and programs, however, is almost non-existent. This fact seriously complicates the spiritual renewal of the local congregation.

20.

Global
Perspective and Concern
Are Missing

There is a delicate balance between focusing on the spiritual needs of individuals and demonstrating a concern for the whole world. Each Christian must see how he personally fits into his church, how his local church is a part of the Christian community and how the Christian action on the local level becomes a vital part of the church universally. A great handicap to the local effort has been a leap-frog approach to the world mission of the church. A perennial interest in foreign fields is maintained without demonstrating adequate concern for the local community.

There is another side to the coin even though the church in general has been preoccupied with foreign evangelism and the "regions beyond." Many local congregations and individual Christians are unable to identify their Christian activity with global Christian objectives. A "come" structure and a "sheep fold mentality" has robbed the church of the "go" strategy. It is obvious then, when the church fails, it fails at the local level.

A great deal of the "foreign concern" is actually an effort to escape responsibility closer home. The women's missionary society and the laymen's league are almost a monastic establishment shut away from the world. They are religious; they are concerned, but concerned about what or who? Themselves mostly, or perhaps the whole world to the exclusion of the most needy cases and the spiritual welfare roles of hometown churches.

Going to the next man, to the next home and into the next town must be an intricate part of Christian outreach strategy. Christians must break out of the encirclement and reach beyond themselves to taste the fruit of evangelism. This activity should be seen as spiritual work and as a vital part of the total ministry of the church universally. Christians should understand that when they are instrumental in reaching one man with the gospel they have, through cooperative action with the Holy Spirit, added to the growing Body of Christ.

Christians must enlarge their concept of membership beyond the sphere of the local church to include themselves as a part of the church universally. Only when this concept is firmly planted in the minds of individuals will they act with global perspective and concern.

The purpose of cooperative action in the church is the winning of souls and the revival of personal commitments to Christ. This can only be accomplished when everyone tells the good news everywhere. Evangelism cannot be left to the pulpit or the preacher; it is the work of the whole church. Every Christian must continually demonstrate genuine concern for the lost.

When everyone is concerned about evangelism the church grows. Growth creates the problems of enlargement. When these problems exist, the church must consider enlarging the program, the building and the staff to meet the greater opportunity. The program must be greater in scope, the building more suitable and the staff more adequate. Outreach contacts require preparation for permanent growth. The fruit harvested in revival and through personal soul winning, must be sheltered, cared for and nurtured by the church.

As the church grows and the vision enlarges, the desire to expand the work of the church becomes more visible.

Normally this expresses itself in strong home missions and foreign missions efforts. New congregations are established. New churches are organized. Pioneer efforts are initiated. New field crusades are considered. Concern for foreign fields becomes apparent as world missions gifts grow. A strong desire to "go into all the world until all have heard the good news" prevails.

As the church expands, the preparation and production of publications must be considered. Leaders must be willing to express their views and publish their opinions. Men willing to lead and to speak out are essential to progress. The action of editorializing crystalizes the thinking of leadership and communicates this thinking into the rank and file. Leaders have a vantage point which often causes them to understand problems better. Knowing their thoughts helps to make others willing to follow.

Remembering those in need is an important part of a mature Christian's life. Neither the church nor an individual Christian can long neglect those in physical need without becoming indifferent about spiritual things. Almsgiving to support works of love among the needy has always been a by-product of the Christian experience. An expression of Christian charity to widows, orphans, the sick and suffering and the neglected members of society is vital if the church is to communicate God's love to the world. Christians should remember the words of Jesus when He identified Himself with the hungry and thirsty stranger in prison saying, "Inasmuch as ye have done it unto one of the least of these my brethren, ye have done it unto me" (Matthew 25:40).

When the church grows larger and becomes involved in programming both for those within the fellowship and those yet unreached, problems of management, administration and finance often hinder the progress. Each Christian must believe that God has the answer to his material needs. This clears the way for regular and systematic support of the church and church-related ministries. Both clergy and congregation must be concerned about the natural causes that affect the operation of the church. This concern causes laymen to involve themselves in both the management of funds and the use of talent. Both are essential to progress.

Re-enlisting the negligent is a major task of the church. Great is the loss of the church occasioned by the indifferent and the inactive. Their absence and in-activity provide an excellent excuse for the unchurched. They are a constant burden to the pastor and a demoralizing influence on active members.

The church must not be too selective in evangelism. Every man must be reached with the gospel regardless of race, culture, language or economic standing. Church-men ought not, by decision or default, leave out any group of people in the outreach ministry. The redeeming blood of Jesus Christ was shed for every tribe, tongue, people and nation. The obligation of the church is to minister and accept as brethren all who confess Christ as Lord. There are large language, cultural and racial groups that are open to the gospel; and the church has an obligation to reach them with the gospel.

While the church ought to be concerned for those outside the fellowship, the church must not neglect the Christian education of the whole church family. Children, young people, adults, must all be considered. This requires a progressive and aggressive program of youth and Christian education. This concern also includes programs of higher education that are academically sound and adequate to prepare young people for professional life. The support of training for pastors, evangelists and Christian teachers should be considered in any general program of education.

The church must aspire to excellence in all aspects of education and evangelism. The concern must be for everyone, everywhere. Only a compassionate look at the whole world can give the church an adequate view of the individual in his true relationship and relative importance. When churchmen become spiritually aware that one soul is worth more than the whole world, they can no longer neglect their personal involvement in the total church vision.

21.

Church Planting Is Neglected

The local organization often becomes an end in itself, thereby thwarting the natural advance of the church. Spiritual reproduction whether it be of individual Christians or of the Christian community itself is basically the work of the Holy Spirit. Nothing, neither men nor methods, can reproduce the spiritual life of the church; this is the ministry of the Spirit. Since it is basically a work of the Spirit, churchmen often expect an "instant" church to materialize whenever and wherever the need exists. Consequently, the delicate task of planting churches is neglected.[40]

Although God is the force behind dynamic reproduction of spiritual life, God does depend upon men for the advancement of His church. Nothing can eliminate the human effort and the hard work necessary to bring churches into existence. In all the knowledge gained about Christian experience and evangelism, very little has been learned about the science of church-birth. There are no easy formulas or simple ways to plant new churches in the world today. This probably accounts for the whole subject being neglected by most Christian leaders.

The mission to reproduce is given to the church and is the dominating theme of the Book of Acts. The dynamic quality of the Spirit was given to the early disciples for the purpose of multiplying the basic units of the church around the world. The Commission of Christ derives both its meaning and power from this event.

Within the church are the seeds for new churches. As in nature, the church is both the goal and the means of reproduction. Churchmen, however, seem to confuse the goal with the means. Christ established the goal toward which all evangelistic purpose of the church is to be directed. His language is clear: "I will build my church and the gates of hell shall not prevail against it." The goal then is cooperation with the program of Christ to reach people who in turn become a part of the Christian fellowship. Christians are to be both the saved and the saving influence in the world.

Information about the essential mission of the church has been increasing. Hundreds of churches have multiplied in different societies, languages and cultures and the means of propagating the gospel used in these areas can be learned. The world mission of the church may now be guided not only by the timeless truths of Scripture, but also by the experience of the past and the effective programs of the present.

Proclaiming Christ and multiplying churches in various parts of the world is a different task. Europe and America are different and the other parts of the world are different from these two basic areas of the Christian community. A denomination must look at the kind of church existing in each area, including the regional areas of the USA, if it is to properly program for these churches or plant new ones.

Many churches are young and each church in each region of a country is at a different stage of development. It is vital to understand how churches grow in the specific population to which God is directing the church to move. Churchmen must stop spending years exploring dead-end roads. Planting churches involves many delicate operations each suitable in a specific kind of society. A good place to begin is to examine the causes of failures and ask what procedures God has blessed.

‵Many moves of God are unplanned. The church must tend the fires that are started by the Holy Spirit. The New Testament shows, however, that the expansion of the gospel was not normally left to spontaneous unintentional growth. God has a better plan. Paul consciously determined to transform the unplanned outreach to the Gentiles into planned movements. His thinking must have been influenced by his time in Antioch working with Greek and Hebrew "Christians." There is no record of Paul converting Gentiles (Galatians 1:6; Acts 26:17) or planting Gentile churches until after the Antioch experience. Paul understood from Antioch how he was going to carry out his commission "to preach Christ among the Gentiles." The Holy Spirit guided his strategy by determining which Gentiles were prepared for the gospel.[41] ╱

The probable outreach of the Antioch Church was through kinsmen. There must have been relatives in Cyprus, Pesedia, Iconium, Lystra and Derbe. Relatives were scattered all over the known world. The last chapter of Romans sheds light on Paul's advance information. Paul had never been to Rome, but he had half a dozen relatives there and knew at least twenty-six people by name.[42]

Through the Spirit and through available knowledge Paul selected the soil in which he sowed the gospel seed. He used responsive groups as bridges. Paul and his friends moved within the bond of relationship to bring their kinsmen to the Christian faith. Paul simply followed up groups of people who were ready for Christian harvest. This may explain his desire to go to Spain (Romans 15:26).[43]

Only once did Paul preach to unattached Gentiles—his address on Mars' Hill—and it does not seem to have planted a church. Paul no doubt won many unattached Gentiles to Christ. However, the few references to conversion among unattached Gentiles do not name a single convert who became influential in the church. New churches came mainly from inside the circle of preconditioned contacts.[44]

The New Testament clearly shows an unplanned overflow of Christianity into the Greek community (Antioch), but also the New Testament clearly demonstrates a planned strategy of intentional labors where Paul deliberately followed responsive groups and expanded existing interest in Christianity.

Churchmen must become competent in the science of mission. The church cheats itself if it does not provide practical understanding of the problems. The church has a divine mission; it is also big business. It takes effort to keep it running smoothly, raising the money needed, recruiting new leadership, solving problems as they rise, keeping the whole undertaking financially responsible and spiritually blessed. These are all a part of the task, but only a part. The whole church organization exists to propagate the Christian faith. To neglect the planting of new churches can be fatal to the spiritual vitality of any congregation.

The work of the church is being carried on in the midst of tremendous revolution affecting every aspect of human life. The guidelines and assumptions under which pioneers and Christian ministers worked have been altered greatly by society. Advances in knowledge changed many political alignments. The vastly accelerated secularization of society, presents the church with radically new ground on which to operate. Men must be prepared to propagate the Christian faith in the new world as it is born.

One basic problem with churchmen in planting new units is the confusion of activity and objective. Oftentimes evangelistic activity is confused with evangelistic objectives. This brings the problem back to the goal and the means. Converts are the objective. Bringing these converts into Christian fellowship and equipping them for Christian service is the spiritual activity essential to initiating a new congregation. The special gifts and special training necessary to do this work is often overlooked.

The church neglects adequate preparation of men charged with the responsibility of planting churches. A close look at a New Testament pattern illustrated in I Thessalonians 1:1-4 is a good place to start. Obviously, there was a team effort when Paul, Silas and Timothy came to Thessalonica. A togetherness in Christ was developed as converts were brought into Christian fellowship. The leadership continued in intercessory prayer for their converts as the Spirit reminded them of the activity that faith inspired, the labor that love prompts and the endurance that hope brings to the heart of converts.

In addition to this, the ministers had full knowledge that God loved each man and had a place for him in kingdom work. When these basic elements are combined with the preaching of the gospel, the preachers faith can be reproduced, the gospel can have impact on the people, then there will be a transforming witness that becomes a cohesive force binding converts together in worship and evangelism.

Food, Fun and Fellowship

(Fellowship-Centered Problems)

As the church concentrates on a narrow definition of fellowship, a "no harvest" theology grows. Many activities have no soul winning objective. The church seems to concentrate on keeping the constituency happy. This precipitates a "come" strategy where the church opens the doors and waits for the people. Since fellowship is not strong enough to hold any group together, an active constituency drift exists that is usually concealed by statistics. In an effort to seek and maintain fellowship with a denomination, conference or material supply source, churches adjust their program and activities to maintain a connection with a parent group. This produces a paternalism that often prevents local problem solving and causes an over dependency on external assistance. The problems of fellowship also wall-in converts and isolate them from their potential. It also causes the church constituency to place priority on secondary projects and often is responsible for individuals being lost in the crowd.

22. A "No Harvest" Theology Grows
23. A "Come" Strategy Prevails
24. An Active Constituency Drift Is Concealed
25. Paternalism Prevents Local Problem Solving
26. Walls Isolate Converts from Their Potential
27. Priorities Are Given to Secondary Projects
28. Individuals Are Lost in the Crowd

22.

A
"No Harvest" Theology
Grows

As the church concentrates on a narrow definition of fellowship a "no harvest" theology grows. Many activities have no soul winning objective. They are designed only to keep the constituency happy. Meeting-centered activities prevail. Groups meet and talk. The usual consensus is "something must be done!" But very little is done other than appoint a committee and schedule another meeting to eat or talk. The personal conviction and conclusion "I must do something" is seldom reached. The logical sequence to "I must" is "I can do all things through Christ . . . "

What has happened to the passion that persuaded men to evangelize in the first century? What supplied the zeal that made it unnecessary for the epistles to repeat the commission? The "go ye" was placed in the heart of every convert and they were anxious to tell the "good news." Somehow in the process of splitting theological hairs, men lost the appreciation for personal confrontation. This caused Christians to retreat into the protective fellowship of the group and finally brought about a stagnation and thrust the church into a nonproductive role in the world.

The church must keep a New Testament harvest theology to be adequate. Remember in Luke 15 the sheep, the coin, and the lost son were all *found*. Men have their role of planting seed and watering but "God causes the miracle of growth" (I Corinthians 3:4-9). The question here is not the work or the workers, but who gets the credit. Men are God's agents. A farmer does not plant for the exercise or experience. He plants with an eye to the harvest. He plans and counts the harvest in advance. He uses selected fields. He abandons fields (soils) that do not produce. He stops plowing rocky fields that break plows and produces a poor harvest. Churchmen must also think as a farmer and maintain an adequate harvest theology.[45]

The readiness of men to receive help when met at their point of need means the church can grow tremendously. The magnitude of this opportunity for growth cannot be clearly illustrated because many churchmen expect slow growth and often feel that rapid growth is somehow discreditable. This causes churchmen to limit their activities to preparing people to someday accept Christ. The church should be engaged in instructing and initiating converts, organizing new units, and training leaders. This is the continuing task of evangelism.

There is no end to the growth of the church that steps out on faith and concentrates on a central idea: that of going everywhere and preaching the gospel with assurance that the Lord will confirm His Word by attending results—spiritual growth. This method was valid in New Testament days and is still God's way for advancing Christianity. Church growth still depends on making disciples, not just an increase in numbers.

The challenge is not to maintain the status quo but to reach out by faith to the unchurched multitudes and even to the "churched" who have a sincere longing for true New Testament involvement. Today's opportunities can be seen in true dimension only when Christians fully grasp the impact and pattern of New Testament outreach.

The Bible furnishes ample precedent for a personalized

and persistent program of outreach and growth. Not only the authoritative examples in the early church, but churchmen are also confronted on the contemporary scene with adequate churches that are constantly being strengthened and enlarged through a personalized program of outreach.

The best results in evangelism are produced through a systematic effort; however, it is evident that even spasmodic ventures in "people-to-people" efforts have proved to be a tremendous growth factor. The active participation of laymen in a structured and internally motivated program of outreach furnishes a church with new fervor for New Testament evangelism and an important fact becomes clear: God uses men to carry His message to the lost. The objective of New Testament growth can be easily summarized in one word—souls.

God has great plans for His church. Phillips translates Ephesians 1:5: "He planned in His purpose of love, that we should be adopted as His own children through Jesus Christ . . . " " . . .because of the great love He had for us," Paul says in Ephesians 2:5; "He gave us life together with Christ . . ." Phillips translation of Ephesians 3:9-11 speaks clearly of God's purpose, that it was " . . . to make plain to all men, the meaning of that divine secret which He who created everything has kept hidden from the creation until now. The purpose is that all the angelic powers should now see the complex wisdom of God's plan being worked out through the Church, in conformity to that timeless purpose which He centered in Christ Jesus, our Lord."

In basic evangelism, the fellowship and excitement of a crowd is still a real problem. Some think that no one can be an "evangelist" unless he beats a big drum. A man who is persuasively pleasing and personally charming seems to be the required trademark of God's "big names." Individual Christians must be willing to face the music on this score. God does not look at the organization or promotion behind a man before He decides to bless his efforts. God looks inside the man. Only this determines God's blessings. No individual believer has to play second fiddle to the big names in evangelism. God has commissioned the church—this includes every born-again believer.

This may be a wicked day in human history, but what a day of opportunities for Christians. Churches must not limit activities to preparing people to someday accept Christ. Spiritual harvest is a NOW thing. A change of attitude is necessary to create an atmosphere conducive to growth. The church must alter concepts of building, program and people to be adequate in this day.

The antiquated idea that the task of operating a church means working without commensurate growth of the church should be blotted out. Every activity, practice and function of the church should have as its immediate goal the evangelism of the lost and the Christian education of believers.

This does not mean that every local congregation of the church will grow constantly, because there are areas where existing conditions demand constant labor to hold present gains. Even in New Testament days when the church grew so rapidly there were areas that seemed to be untouched by the gospel.

During the years 33 A.D. to 48 A.D. the number of Christians in Judea grew enormously. Yet, their message did not touch Phoenicia right next door to Judea; and even though the gospel was proclaimed by the incomparable Paul himself among the Gentiles of Syria and Cilicia, there was little, if any, response worth mentioning in the New Testament account.

There are areas of little response and consequently small opportunity for church growth. There are also areas of great response and large opportunities for growth. The church must be concerned with those areas where the gospel is readily accepted and where the greatest number of souls can be won. Only then can the church be considered a good steward of the present opportunity afforded for growth and outreach.

When Paul heard that the Holy Spirit was bringing

Gentiles to discipleship in Antioch, he promptly left Tarsus and went to Antioch. He was going where the church had opportunity to grow. When Spirit-filled Christians witness with confidence, the mysterious action of God grips hearts who have a sense of desperate need—this creates converts that are ready to serve Christ and His cause.

It is God's will that His church grow. Not only does He want the local church to grow, He wants it to be fruitful and multiply and start new churches. The local church is the essential unit and the individual believer is the adequate instrument for world evangelism. Each church and each believer has the innate capacity to grow and reproduce itself. This is God's plan.

No other institution or organization on earth has Christ as its official head. This should inspire the beleaguered church as it looks to the Author and the Finisher of this fight against sin and evil. As "the body of Christ" the church has the willing assistance of the Godhead. Christ as the head and each member fitly joined together in spiritual union is the great potential of the church on earth. The lack of emphasis of this aspect of the church probably accounts for the haphazard attitude that both clergy and laity take about the function of the body. Man needs more than fellowship to stay alive. So does the church.

The New Testament church had an automatic ability to grow and progress. The characteristics were very akin to the sprouting and the growing process of a living seed. Man can plant and water. God must do the rest. New Testament growth cannot be created, it can only be influenced, shaped, slowed or accelerated. Man also has a role in the growing of a functioning body. Scriptures indicate that the body grows from the head through the natural channels according to special laws which God has laid down for living things. To be effective, the church must maintain a strategy for growth and harvest that does not impede natural dynamics but constantly creates a climate conducive to normal growth.

One of the problems with the church today as a living body is that it has many disassociated functions and manifestations that cannot be identified as a part of the living organism. When each part does not harmoniously contribute to growth the church is in trouble. Often today, personal competition and striving for position frustrates the natural function of the body. Routine church administration fails to recognize this fact and places the church into an awkward and unproductive state.

The church as a growing body has at least two basic functions. There is a growth by increasing the size and a growth by multiplying the number. These functions are interrelated and almost inseparable. It is almost impossible to have effective growth without efficient operation of each aspect of the basic function. This is true because these are the essential manifestations of a living and growing body.

Oftentimes the growth pattern of the church is frustrated because men look for only one aspect of growth, a growth in numbers. Since the church is mistakenly thought of in terms of an assembly of people, many people seem to be preoccupied with "noses and nickels." The aspects of nurture and the improvement of quality are often overlooked. Growth takes place when the human element maintains the body in a state of spiritual health and permits the Spirit to move on the lives of individuals. This brings about the rapid growth and reproduction essential for maintaining both life and vitality.

Some see the church as a holy club or spiritual retreat for men beleaguered by urban society. They do not see the church as an active and contributing part of the big city. This is inexcusable because the New Testament was a world of cities. Twenty-three cities are significant in its pages. Except for parts of Christ's Galilean ministry and perhaps some happenings on the road, the whole action of the New Testament takes place in an urban environment. Thus, a New Testament type church is relevant and assumes a dynamic dimension of usefulness in today's urbanized society.

The gospel was adequate for the city dweller of New Testament days. A New Testament strategy for cities works today. It is a simple plan of person-to-person evangelism. Set at the crossroads of trade, cosmopolitan in nature, with deep-rooted tradition, the pagan cities of the New Testament knew all the problems of New York and London. Yet, the gospel was adequate for all who believed.

The implication for a city strategy is obvious. God has promised a surge of spiritual vitality in the "last days." Joel's children will witness effectively to all flesh. The mission station concept must be discarded with a thousand and one other "more modern means." The church needs the same gospel—the same answer because man's problem has not changed. While the church seeks for new solutions to the age old problem of sin, the adequacy of the simple gospel message is neglected. God's simple plan still works. Without a New Testament harvest theology the church can never win the world.

23.

A
"Come" Strategy
Prevails

When a congregation begins, it is usually initiated by persons who know one another and share the common desire to give birth to a church. The strategy for coming together is based on this willingness to participate, but once the church has organized itself into a fellowship of believers this strategy should be altered.

Many congregations never outgrow this early family concept of the church. It is natural for family members to return home and for children to be born into the family during the normal course of the year. Certainly the church can grow in the same way, but this alone is not adequate. Nonetheless, a "come" strategy is prevalent in most congregations today.

This is a problem of quantitative static.[47] The church opened the doors and waited for the people, but they never came. Growth ceased because soul winning stopped. Many in the community remain unchurched and the majority have not been significantly influenced by the Christian experience to be classified as believers. Yet, many church leaders insist on playing the waiting game. Meanwhile, things continue as usual.

As the religious life of such a church becomes organized, pastoral care becomes a regular part of the church ministry and the congregation becomes passive about growth and progress. Regular services are scheduled and the pastor is very active in programming for his constituency. Members attend church regularly and receive reports of the ministry and programs of the church but do not, themselves, become actively involved in any evangelistic outreach. They develop a philosophy of "come to see us if you can, but if you don't come, we'll manage without you."

The constituency of such a church desires a degree of outreach and recognizes the need to evangelize, but somehow, they feel that they have employed a minister to do their work. They occasionally send for a special guest to beef-up the interest in the program but there is little, if any, personal involvement. The church frequently will send part of their group to participate in evangelism elsewhere. They seem pleased when their young men desire to enter the ministry or when someone feels that his life work should be on some foreign field. They even have a prayerful concern for evangelists and missionaries, but can never see their personal responsibility beyond a prayer concern for others. Their evangelistic obligation is only "burden bearing" in terms of prayer and with no personal participation.

This lack of individual involvement is difficult to understand when pockets of paganism remain on every side of the church. Whole families who have not been influenced by the Christian message are within a stone's throw of the church building. Many parts of the city do not have churches or actively witnessing Christians. Such a church and its constituency may be actively concerned about world missions and home extension programs of a denomination or conference but usually turn a deaf ear to the cry of evangelism at their door. Both clergy and congregation are satisfied to settle for a co-existence with an unchurched and unChristian community. When this happens the evangelistic growth ceases and the church becomes static in its quantitative growth.

This indifferent resignation to the presence of unconverted souls extinguishes the last spark of evangelistic fervor within the congregation. Church members are active in the community, mixing daily with non-Christians in their work and social exchange. They participate jointly with the community in organized civil and social functions, yet they seem to be completely unaware of the opportunities for daily witness. If an awareness is present, they show no sense of obligation or responsibility to participate in the work of ministering to the needs of men.

The congregation continues to be concerned for the gospel in faraway places and maintains a deep and sincere interest in the material progress of the local church. Yet they seem totally unconcerned about the spiritual needs of men about them. With little or no awareness of what has happened, the church settles down to a quiet life of coexistence with the world.

In fact, such a church becomes so concerned with the little family group that new blood or fresh ideas from the world outside would become a threat to the easy-going conciliatory approach that has developed. Without being concious of the problem, they develop an obvious attitude toward the outside world, close akin to a "send them away" philosophy. A church will be located there for many years to come. The attendance will remain the same but the church is static and will not grow unless they can shed the "come" strategy complex that prevails in the minds and hearts of both the pastor and the membership.

Growth in numbers is a good test as to whether Christians really have the mind of Christ.[48] Growth is essential for normal life. There are two major aspects of church growth: quantity, a growth in numbers; and quality, a growth in maturity and spirituality. Both are essential to the advancement of the church, but at times each has priority. When a congregation is small, when the regular worship service is attended by only a handful, the priority should be numbers. However, when the present building is filled to capacity the priority should be spiritual development and growth that leads to new and major steps for growth.

Solitary Christians or small bands of separated Christians can and do exist when held together by a deep love for Christ and one another; but if they do not gather to themselves a community sufficiently large to provide social requirements, marriage companions for their children, et cetera, they live a partial life and their survival through the generations is doubtful.

Many decry the call for numerical increase. This challenge to numerical growth is entirely sound; yet it is distasteful to some Christians who constantly praise spiritual growth. To many, numerical growth is mechanical and neglects spiritual development. However, numerical growth is essential to progress! This does not condone roll-padding or statistic hungry ministers who stop at nothing to have good "reports."

McGavran makes it clear that "numerical growth presupposes and necessitates good spiritual care." Men turn to the churches who have a program and ministry suited to their needs. True, some may be encouraged by friends and relatives to come to church, but they will not remain there unless they receive real food for thought and spiritual help with their daily lives. Newcomers must feel that their life has been changed for good; that they are better men and enjoy a life superior to the one they had before, otherwise they would neither come in nor stay. It is clearly evident that a church whose program suits the actual needs of its congregation has the basic framework for adequacy. Other factors must be taken into account but this is essential.[49]

The magnitude of the present opportunity cannot be clearly seen because most churchmen have labored under the false premise that church growth will be slow and rather disappointing and often feel that rapid growth is somehow discreditable. The church must take com-

mand of a major idea—valid in New Testament days—
that of going everywhere and preaching the Word expecting the Lord to confirm His Word with miraculous
growth. The "come" strategy must go if the church
is to grow.

24.

An Active
Constituency Drift
Is Concealed

Many older and larger churches camouflage their lack of growth by statistics and materialistic veneer on the church building complex. From all appearance they have "a name that they live but they are dead." These congregations most likely inherited the problem from their parents. Being a second- or third-generation church, they fall heir to false concepts and stereotyped methods.

The "come" strategy that sapped the evangelistic fervor and the "send them away" philosophy that isolated the congregation from the community requires a professionalism to create an image of progress. The church becomes preoccupied with the secondary. Instead of spending time in outreach ministry, they are concentrating on counting "noses and nickels" and involving themselves in professional and prestige problems.

There is an active spiritual drift within the congregation of which the church is unaware.[50] The range of membership spans the distance from committed Christians to nominal Christians. The active core of committed Christians forms a nucleus and devotional group who maintains a semblance of spiritual life within the congregation. At the other end of the axes would be the nominal members who are Christian in name only and are associated with the church for social, business or personal advantage. Many in the congregation are really marginal believers and remain on the fringe of activity and on the outer most perimeter of involvement.

A slow but active drift of committed Christians towards an average or marginal position is present but not always evident. Average church members drift toward nominality. Because of the nucleus of committed Christians and the number of average or marginal people that remain involved in the program of the church, the drift in the congregation often goes unnoticed. The first major symptom of the problem is when the same persons are involved in the leadership of most all the activities of the church.

The average and marginal membership of the congregation have little or no opportunity for active participation and drift slowly but surely toward a nominal position. The congregation may be strong in numbers and in material wealth but it is suffering from qualitative static. There is little spiritual development within the congregation. The church badly needs a spiritual renewal program to bring the average and marginal members face to face with a fresh Christian commitment. The spiritual leadership of the church spends a majority of its time and energy in a constant effort to move membership toward the committed end of the spectrum. In spite of this, a drift in the opposite direction continues.

Tragic as these problems may seem in an enlightened age, the real difficulty lies in the lack of evangelistic outreach. The new generation, unconverted and uninvolved, is never reached, yet the older and mature membership is lost constantly due to death and spiritual mortality. Since the church does not reach the new generation, it is destined to a gradual but certain death.

The congregation may have inherited the seed problem from parents and the previous generation. The problem seems to be perpetuated by the pulpit. Often the content of the message is non-Biblical and deals with the whims and anxieties of man but has no spiritual basis for a recovery of lost faith. Often the message is watered down to eliminate the elements which might be offensive to the uncommitted congregation. Much of the preaching is secular, unauthentic and false in terms of New Testament validity. The pulpit constantly nags the people into doing good and attempts to motivate and attract participation in the social improvement of the community.

The Holy Spirit must be permitted to prepare both the preacher to minister and the church to hear the preached Word. The Word of God speaks to individuals only after the Spirit has created an atmosphere of reverence and respect. The minister's New Testament responsibility is clear: prayer and study of the Word. However, he spends most of his time in administration, programming, attending meetings, making pastoral calls or community service. He leaves little or no time for honest toil in the ministers workshop.

The problem lies primarily with the faith of the preacher. Since he does not live within the framework of the faith he proclaims, his pulpit ministry is not taken seriously. The clergy has found a way to separate religion from life. There is a problem of an "integrity crisis" that demonstrates itself regularly and produces serious spiritual and theological problems for the congregation. Some preachers are more concerned about their personal popularity than they are about the proclamation of truth. The dilemma of many churches today stems from a concern for the pulpit and the preacher at the expense of a genuine concern for the gospel itself. Men are more concerned about popularity and fellowship.

The question is constantly asked, "If the purpose of preaching is to produce action, change lives and make new lives in the community, why do we not see more fruits of that action?" There are no simple answers. The problem is more persuasive and demands serious study of communication problems and the new situation in which the preacher lives and ministers. However, the crisis must be identified as a preaching crisis since faith comes by hearing and hearing by the Word of God. The responsibility lies directly on the shoulders of the preachers.

Fellowship is not strong enough to hold any group together. Only the cohesive force of the Holy Spirit and the Word are adequate to bind a congregation together in Christ. Only a pulpit of power can enlighten men to spiritual solutions and to spiritual problems. No amount of camouflage programming or statistical manipulation can make a weak church strong or a bad report good. It is disastrous and criminal to try.

Conscientious Christians should tell it like it is. The church must face the facts about the inadequacy of both form and function. Churchmen must tell the truth because anything that creates a sense of desperate need on the part of individuals opens the door to evangelism and church growth. The challenge is to make use of present opportunities and to discipline responsive souls into stalwart Christian leaders to further the cause of Christ.

25.

Paternalism
Prevents
Local Problem Solving

Small churches are plagued by many problems but most of them are caused by a special kind of paternalism.[51] Their conduct is regulated and most of their needs are supplied by outside sources. The church has made preliminary and minor arrangements concerning their local financial operation and have harvested the ready fields immediately available to them. Yet, somehow the congregation has no desire to direct its own affairs. The church has been crippled by a resignation to paternalism.

In an effort to seek and maintain corporate fellowship with a denomination, conference or even a materials supply source, many churches adjust their program and activities to maintain connection with the parent group. This has many advantages and contributes a great deal to the welfare of new congregations, but there are some limitations. The uniformity of co-operative programming presupposes the same needs and resources everywhere. Rather than gearing a program to local needs, generalizations are necessary that weaken local effectiveness of the programs. This often produces a special kind of paternalism that prevents local problem solving and stifles creative initiative. Consequently, church leadership and the congregation as a whole become overly dependent on external assistance.

There is little creative programming within the congregation. Someone else makes decisions for them and they willingly abide by these decisions. There is no initiative within the hearts and minds of the local constituency to tailor a program to the local needs. Even though the program may not be understood, they still attempt with all diligence to participate in denominational and conference projects, and strive earnestly for a good report. The preacher and the congregation both seem subservient to a bishop or superintendent and most of their energies go into efforts to please ecclesiastical hierarchy. A spirit of cooperation is good, but striving to please men can never create an atmosphere conducive to New Testament growth.

In many small congregations the natural capacity of the congregation has remained untapped. The leadership and organizational initiative that could be brought to bear on church and community problems never seem to emerge. Stewardship initiative is choked because of a constant request for goals and projects alien and foreign to the knowledge and understanding of the local constituency rather than being motivated by an internal desire to assist someone whom they know personally. They continue to bow to generalizations. The church may send a bicycle to missionary "what's his name" or build a small village church for "somebody somewhere," but there seems to be no personal involvement or internal motivation. Most of the stewardship efforts and participation comes because of pressure from the parent body rather than from a genuine willingness to be involved.

The small church remains small because it usually avoids financial obligations well within its economic capacity. Since individual initiative and resources have not been developed, the small church lacks the will to venture unless it can be underwritten by some larger parent body. To grow, a church must have indigenous goals that include self-support, self-determination and self-propagation. A cooperative spirit of fellowship must remain, but should not be the cause for neglecting personal and local needs. Most churches have the potential in education, in personnel and in physical resources for achieving local goals. Yet somehow paternalism robs the congregation of the ability to "grow up" and they suffer from over-protection. Often the leadership, and the congregation as well, act and react very childishly and become resigned to a state of dependence on a paternally oriented program.

There is nothing wrong with a centralized government or groups of churches agreeing on a doctrinal position and accepting general denominational goals and cooperative programming. This is a logical framework for progress. However, unless conferences and groups of churches build into their program a measure of self-discipline and local initiative, progress remains at a minimum. The denomination may be anxious to stimulate growth, but because of past paternalistic attitudes the local church level remains the same and the denomination, as well as the local group, becomes a victim of organic static. They simply remain as they are, never altering program or policy to meet the need of contemporary society. No spiritual or physical progress is visible. The church simply remains a "mission station."

No one will argue the fact that change is necessary in this day. But this does not mean doctrine or principles must change. The New Testament ethic remains valid. It only means that the application of certain practical aspects of the ministry must be rechanneled into workable programs. The objective of organized groups of churches is by and large the same. They wish to believe the same thing and practice the same thing and basically want the local church to be financially secure enough to meet contemporary needs at the local level. After all, the vitality of the local church is the only hope for progress.

This is an age of speedy change. Unless local churches emerge from the over-protected, over-programmed policies and become locally and internally motivated, very little progress can be accomplished. Local initiative must be brought to bear against the reality of local problems. Laymen and clergy alike must encounter the contemporary problems of their society, make local decisions, develop their own financial responsibilities and, to some degree, become aware of their own self-hood. When this happens, the church can be dynamic and reach its full potential.

The church can grow adequately only in a dynamic situation. Everything must change but the doctrine. Even the doctrine must have new applications to each generation. A church cannot grow unless it is fed from within. When any congregation stops within the process of growing and developing, it is underfed within. It has lost its evangelical outreach and fails to emerge as a growing entity. When this happens it is vulnerable to all kinds of disease and difficulty.

The problems of paternalism can be overcome only at the grass root level. Pastors and lay leaders must take charge and become the active agents of local progress. Clergy and laity alike must be thoroughly trained in Biblical principles and in ways and means of communicating to contemporary man. They must be prepared for personal and group encounter within their own cultural environment. They must know how to interpret the theology of the New Testament and translate it into the daily situation. They must somehow shed the tendency to split theological hairs or raise controversial questions. To be adequate, leadership must be established on the local scene, identifying culturally with the people they are to serve. This will cause them to constantly stress the validity and vitality of the local church.

Each generation must be won to Christ individually.

Often it is necessary to re-win certain individuals within each generation. The church has a continuing obligation for a successive harvest. No generation can live on the experience of its predecessor or beyond doctrinal principles, nor be unduly influenced by the program and practices of the previous generation and expect to grow. Most problems encountered by the local congregation can be traced directly to erroneous assumptions based on a false pride and loyalty to policies of the past.

Growth within the fellowship and spiritual initiative within the lives of leadership and constituency can bring about evanglistic outreach. The church must not be content to win its own; it must see the entire new generation as potential converts. This includes children of parents who do not associate themselves with the church. Each generation is searching for someone to follow and some cause worthy of a lifetime commitment. It is the obligation of the church to point them to Christ, His teachings and the practical aspects of Christian living. When a church becomes involved in the winning of individuals to the cause of Christ, they cannot lethargically or indifferently resign themselves to dependence on anyone but God and the spiritual enablement given to meet the needs of the world around them.

Research in the field of psychology points directly to solutions of individual problems. It is quite clear that when an individual has the intellectual aptitude to frame or understand the question, he has the academic capacity to find the answer. It is evident, therefore, that individuals dedicated to God and concerned about the ongoing program of the church can find workable solutions to the problems they face in their personal relationship with God and in their personal involvement in the work of the church.

Sociologists also have researched the problem of the group. They make it clear that when a group together can identify a problem, the group has the capacity to find the answer. Outsiders may offer recommendations, may even suggest solutions, but the real problem solving takes place within the group itself. Every believer should present his part of the solution. Thus, each man becomes part of the answer until consensus puts together a knowledge that individually could not have been achieved. This knowledge produces a workable solution that the majority can accept. The problem and the answer both become clear. Each Christian, whether he be clergy or laity, is either part of the problem or he is part of the answer. Only total church involvement in local problem solving can chart a course for progress and growth.

26.

Walls Isolate Converts From Their Potential

The problems of fellowship seem to wall in converts and isolate them from their soul winning potential. Some churches constantly separate converts from their potential by walls of isolation. Others fail to create an awareness of witnessing opportunities. Converts are separated from the world to such a degree that they are isolated from both friend and foe. Those churches that do not maintain strict separation, anesthetize converts to the degree they feel no sensitivity or responsibility for witnessing to the lost. Both extremes are evident. The Christian life is neither staying out of trouble through total separation or minding one's own business and never getting involved with the needs of others. To be Christian, one must be involved.[52]

The Christian life is positive virtue flowing out of the regenerate core of the heart of man. Therefore, sanctification is more than mere abstinance, it is the Lordship of Christ and the rule of the Spirit. It issues in love, kindness and compassion and good works humbly done. Therefore, there can be no detailed regulation of daily situations. The principle force for Christian witness must be in the heart.[53]

Mere mechanical imitation of Christ cannot produce discipleship. Christians are not sheer imitators of Christ; they are partakers of His divine nature. Believers are "sons of God," and "joint heirs with Christ," who participate in the work of God in the world. Peter uttered a universal prayer when he asked that men "might be partakers of the divine nature." Man has a capacity within his nature for the likeness of God. It is possible to be so united and related to Christ that His strength becomes the believer's strength for daily living.

Extremes either way can never accomplish Christ's purpose for believers in the world. Christ loved His followers and wanted them to be in heaven where He was but He earnestly prayed to the Father in John 17 that His followers not be "taken out of the world" but that they be "kept from the evil." This is the problem. The church either keeps them out of the world, which is contrary to the wishes of Christ, or permits participation in the evil of the world, which is also contrary to Christ's prayer.

Paul made it clear in Corinthians that men should "abide in the calling" wherein they are called. Paul wished for men to remain in their present position or occupation as long as it was not immoral and to make use of their connections and contacts for evangelism. John the Baptist, in Luke's gospel, also made it clear that the tax gatherer could remain on his job but that he must be honest. He answered the soldiers' questions and never suggested that they should cease to be soldiers. They were told to avoid violence and false accusation and to be content with their wages. Both John and Paul suggested that believers should remain involved in the work-a-day world, yet keep themselves separated from the sins of the world. Becoming a Christian does not mean that one must desert his friends; it only means that he must separate himself from their sins.

If the church is to win the world, ways must be found to involve new converts immediately in the program of evangelism. Since being a witness is living a life in contrast to one's contemporaries, it is obvious that the new convert can be the greater witness because of the immediate change in his life. It is also evident that a new convert can influence his friends and close associates much easier than anyone else. He has their confidence, he knows their language and he understands their opposition to the gospel because of his immediate past experience. New converts then should be involved in the outreach ministry of the church. Church leaders must be extremely cautious about letting church walls or regulations concerning separation isolate men from their potential soul winning opportunities.

The church must use not only new converts but all of its constituency to create living connections with the unchurched world. Friendship evangelism is still the answer to an impersonal society. Family and friends are much more easily influenced for Christ by intimates who are appreciated for their decision and life for Christ. These are the connections that count in church growth.

A growing church must have living connections.[54] How can these connections be established? The fundamental answer is for each convert to continue a friendly relationship with previous associates. Through the encouragement of mature Christians and the direction of the Spirit, converts can find opportunities to share the message of saving grace. The church has inevitable and unsought involvement within the community, but often there is no program to take advantage of the soul winning opportunities. Encirclement is a basic problem. The very redemption that brings men out of the world causes the church to wall in converts and separate them from those they could reach for Christ and the church.

Church growth of the first magnitude can come only when converts are used immediately to lead their family and friends into a saving knowledge of Christ. New believers must be encouraged to break out of the encirclement and the protection of the church before it becomes binding. Converts must be involved while the enthusiasm of their decision for Christ remains intact and before they become significantly influenced by a lazy and lethargic congregation.

False standards of separation for all practical purposes causes the church to be "absent" from the city. Potential converts are usually approached by the wrong people. This happens because the church permits converts to retreat into the institution and the programs of the church rather than becoming "apostles in the streets." The only way Christianity can remain incarnate in the world is for new converts to be led into an enthusiastic witness to the world. The church must relate to all of life and can only fulfill this obligation when the new constituency is used to produce fruit. In nature, fruit is always a result of new growth. It is the same with the church.

The church must break down the walls and the barriers that hamper the Christian witness in the community. The principle of spontaneous action under the Holy Spirit must be taught. An adequate revelation in Scripture makes clear that New Testament evangelism was based on the Holy Spirit personally directing and guiding each follower of Christ. The Spirit empowered each convert to overcome inhibitions and to speak with boldness the "good news" of the gospel. The church must preach this power. The congregation must be willing to receive the enablement of the Spirit. When the Word of God is preached and the congregation heeds the Word, the ability to persuade men to accept the gospel will be present. The church can then grow because the New Testament dynamics will keep the new converts from becoming isolated from their potential. Soul winning will continue. Christian nurture will continue. Church growth will continue.

Christ was crucified outside the walls of old Jerusalem. Consequently, Christ died for those outside the walls. The Crucifixion outside the walls divorced Christ from the Jewish capital and proclaimed the universality of His redemption and made all men equal before God (Galatians 3:28). This fact, coupled with the torn veil in the temple that had separated the people from the Mercy Seat, is one of the most significant of divine acts recorded in the

Scriptures. True Christianity knows no walls and builds no barriers. Jesus Christ, by His atoning death "broke down the middle wall of partition" that divided mankind. Hostilities ceased (Ephesians 2:14-18).

The genealogy of Jesus reveals a representative of the whole human family. Matthew introduces two women of Gentile birth, Ruth, the Moabitess, and Rahab, the harlot of Jericho, who became women of faith. Tamar and Bathsheba also have questionable records, according to the Old Testament evidence. Christ truly was universal.

The writer of Hebrews reminded converted Jews that Christ died beyond Jerusalem's wall and that the Cross and its benefits were outside the legal jurisdiction of Judaism. They were challenged to break the parochial order and "go forth unto him without the camp, bearing his reproach." Sound advice? Certainly, for shortly Titus (70 A.D.) demolished the walls and destroyed all "within."

Christ tore down walls of prejudices and hatred. He refuted the Temple inside the walls and the Mount Gerazim beyond the walls as a holier place of worship. Christ's death made every place open for worship. Early believers desired to keep Christianity within the framework of Judaism. Some wanted to remain in Jerusalem but God used Saul of Tarsus to scatter them and spread the message. The Christian message was for everyone. Each man had the opportunity of becoming a "selected saint."

The banner of the Cross must be carried beyond every wall, through every barrier and into every heart around the world. True Christianity knows no walls and will recognize none. Any person who claims to belong to Christ but does not go beyond the wall and bear the reproach of Christ must be counted as suspect.

Evidence from around the world is clear that individuals are encouraged in accepting Christ when friends or relatives share their experience and are hindered when they must come alone. Breaking ties with loved ones and friends seems to be almost insurmountable. Social support and fellowship is essential.

Social dislocation at any time is a tragedy.[55] The

kingdom of God is likened unto leaven that spreads throughout the whole. To separate a new convert from his associates is the same as taking the leavening out of the dough. It interferes with his growth and in the growth of the whole. It deprives his former associates of his Christian influence needed to bring them to a saving knowledge of Christ and retards the growth of the church. Every new convert is a potential evangelist provided he grows in grace and becomes an adequate witness.

The church can never grow effectively by extracting individuals from their group. As persons are won to Christ, they should be encouraged to remain within their social group as a witness. The potential for growth here is obvious but is often lost to the church. By separating the convert from his group or social acquaintances, the church sacrifices much evangelistic potential.

All converts separated from the sins of the world by their profession of faith in Christ must be returned to their own friends and relatives as a living example of saving grace. This is the greatest potential for evangelism. In fact, the new convert can more adequately reach his friends than anyone else. Relatives and friends can readily see a change in his life. There is a delicate balance here, a matter of being "in the world" yet not "of the world." But this is what being a Christian witness is all about.

27.

Priorities
Are Given to
Secondary Projects

A major difficulty with the church today is that much of the constituency places priority on secondary projects. The Commission of Christ said nothing about building cathedrals or establishing Christian colleges and seminaries, or sponsoring hospitals, orphanages or asylums or supporting the many other religious and philanthropic causes for which most church personnel concern themselves. These are good and worthy projects and are due careful and prayerful consideration of Christians everywhere, but they are not the primary concern of the church. Yet such projects take most of the time and money of the congregation and as they grow and mature into institutions and social or charitable organizations, they demand more and more of the church's time and money to say nothing of the leadership talent involved.

An objective observer of denominational priorities and anyone who would look closely at the major emphases of the local church could easily determine that the local congregation has become a source of money and personnel to operate programs and projects of a secondary nature.

In fact, where the local church is not involved in outside projects their resources are normally channeled into major building programs and other prestige symbols and civic involvements.

The priority placed on fellowship and social concern is also a threat to the spiritual involvement of most churches. Provided the family and the faithful few are involved in the weekly events of the church, everyone seems to be satisfied. An occasional social or recreational venture to provide an opportunity for "Christian fellowship" is a primary concern of many local programmers.

Another basic problem in reaching people is that leaders are often overtrained. Care must be taken that leadership training does not alienate the leader from his people. When leadership becomes culturally distinctive within the population, the effectiveness of the church is drastically reduced. Key church leadership must be men of the people, men who can identify with the needs and desires of the people.[56]

This is a problem with many churches. Most denominations educate their clergy too far beyond the practical needs of the ministry. In fact, many preachers are educated out of the ministry. Seminary programs often prepare men better for business and industry than for the pulpit.

The most important work of the church today is to fulfill the obligations of the Great Commission. This obligation is simply the business of making disciples. Many of the other things in which the church is involved, the church ought to do. Secondary projects and programs, however, should not be given the priority normally attributed to them. The basic reason for not having a New Testament Church today is that the church cannot accept New Testament priorities: Catching a vision of those who are lost and concentrating all efforts toward evangelization of the masses.

The early church in Jerusalem became preoccupied with fellowship and placed priority on personal welfare and neglected the primary obligation to carry the "good news." Then God sent Saul of Tarsus to stir up their nest through persecution, and scattered them throughout the Roman Empire. Shaken by this drastic move of God, they became aware of individual and personal responsibility. The results were that many were quickly brought into the ranks of Christendom. They became concerned with the primary obligation of reaching every person in their world with the gospel. This is still the Christian's obligation. To be fruitful and adequate a church must seek first things first.

One thing is obvious from church growth research: Men will not cross linquistic or cultural lines to become a Christian. [57] They must be approached within the context of their culture with language easily understood. Yet the church constantly puts priority on the "going" rather than the "making of disciples." Individuals must accept Christ where they are. Once men accept Christ, they can be brought into the fellowship of the church. Men are willing to cross previous barriers to obtain Christian fellowship after conversion.

Social distance is an insurmountable barrier.[58] No one feels "at home" where people and customs are different. Most individuals want to worship with their own kind of people. Churches are most successful where people do not have to cross linguistic, racial or class barriers. It has been suggested that New Testament churches ceased to grow among the Jews when Gentiles became large enough to influence the menu at the Agape Feast. Jews then rejected Christianity because of the Gentile influence.

Some barriers, of course, must be crossed for a person to become a Christian: sin must be confessed and the Cross accepted. However, there is no Biblical or practical basis to force a change of language, class or normal customs (aside from immorality).[59] The church must not demand sanctification as a prerequisite to salvation. Peter at Antioch was rejected by Paul because of the demands of tradition. Keeping tradition is not a prerequisite to receiving Christ as Savior. Christian tradition may well become a part of the believer's life, but only after conversion.

When blacks move into the church or community,

whites simply leave. Most churches do not understand the priorities in this respect. It is not altogether a racial matter. Most of it is a cultural problem and some of it is a spiritual problem. Prejudice is an active part of culture and must be understood if the church is to grow. Cubans and Puerto Rican Christians do not wish to worship together in the same Spanish-speaking churches in New York or Miami because of cultural variations. The same is true of Christians from different parts of the United States. Missionaries report similar difficulties around the world. The variations within a given culture must also be considered if the church is to grow.

One basic priority of the church is prayer—personal prayer. Praying is a powerful thing but even prayer is misunderstood by most Christians. The simple motto: "Prayer Changes Things" is a classic example of how the church has permitted the individual Christian to use and abuse the personal opportunity of prayer. Constantly, churches and Christians everywhere are praying for things to happen, praying for things to change, praying for things to improve. The motto should read: "Prayer Changes People and People Change Things."

Prayer must be personal. If it is initiated and inspired by the Spirit who knows the mind of God, it will be personal. The church must demonstrate a concern for people. Christians must be concerned about individuals. Prayer must be personal to be effective. The fervent prayer of believers avails much when the man is right with God and the Holy Spirit directs his thoughts toward the needs of people.

The great principle of life is that of serving God and others. Everyone soon learns that it is impossible to serve two masters because of conflicting priorities. Therefore, the church as a whole and each individual believer must seek first God's kingdom and His righteousness. The first priority suggests the external aspects of the kingdom. Christians are to seek the spread and accomplishment of God's kingdom in the world. The second priority represents internal aims. Christians are to seek personal conformity to God's standard of right living. Both aspects are fundamental to the whole concept of priority in the Christian Church.

Based upon the principle of service and the priority of obligation, Christians must seek first the kingdom and serve God through a right relationship to their fellowman. The first obligation of human pursuit then is to seek the kingdom of God. This is to seek the rule of God's will in the church and in the world. There are intermediate goals and objectives but priority must be placed on concentrated efforts toward reaching the ultimate objective: winning men to Christ.

Man was made for God—made to love God, made to serve God, made to praise God, made to live in fellowship with God, made to do His will on earth. Priority then is kingdom work and right living and all the other things God will provide. By putting Christ and the kingdom of God first and seeking after His righteousness, men lay the foundation for success in all areas of human endeavor. Without this priority, no congregation of people can be adequate as a church or effective in performing the spiritual ministry in the world. To be preoccupied with secondary things in a time of desperate need is utterly futile for the church and the world.

28.

Individuals Are Lost in the Crowd

A basic problem of the church is that no one programs for the individual. Each individual is a child of his own age and culture and must be understood in the context of his personal needs. However, his personal needs are bound up with the needs of the group to which he belongs and to the community of which he is a aprt. The church must understand both society as a whole and the role of the individual within the group. Otherwise the individual becomes lost in the crowd.

An adequate understanding of the moral and spiritual climate of the group is essential to reaching the individual. The general characteristics of this age are conformity and the "lonely crowd." The space age brought with it an awareness of the immensity of the universe that almost overwhelms the human mind. Doubt is fostered as to the significance of the individual. How could God be concerned about such a small part of the universe? Is man just a cosmic accident or a conglomeration of atoms? These questions plague the minds of men today and must be answered by the church.

This materialistic age is primarily concerned with physical and emotional things. The scientific process and logic have been substituted for revelation and faith. Science has become the God of modern man and has chained the human race to the assembly line and the computer. A current rootless materialism has produced a "cut-flower civilization." Man has become an anonymous, secular something that lives a life of practical atheism. The church is not expressing adequate concern for man's present dilemma.

Some concern has always been expressed for the needs of man. It is interesting to note the evolution of this concern. Initially, it began as a concern for one soul. The realization that one soul was worth more than the whole world caused Christians to structure their mission to reach individuals. The church then became interested in families. The goal was to make church a family affair. Then the concern moved on to include the community, the city, the nation and now the church seems to be preoccupied with a concern for the whole world. This is commendable but inadequate for evangelism because soul winning is a personal matter. The church must get back to the basics: concern for individuals.

The church ought to demonstrate concern for the whole world but a concern for individuals is essential. Men are born one at a time and lost individually. They must be saved one at a time. Knowing the community enables the church to structure a program to reach individuals. The program of the church must be geared to reach individuals within the context of their group. Men must be reached as members of a group, but they are individuals.

The church has failed to become personal in its concern for the world. While the church is preoccupied with society as a whole, or with faraway places with strange sounding names, individuals remain lost. Many of each generation with talent, skill and motivation could have been recruited into the army of the Lord. Yet these unreached remained vocal for causes that destroy man's peace of mind.

Christians in America must accept some degree of responsibility for the great World Wars because they failed to win the future leaders of Germany, Japan and Italy. Most of the key men were educated outside their country. Somehow during the course of two, four or even six years, the church failed to show adequate interest in the spiritual needs of these men. They returned home disillusioned with the American ideal and busied themselves setting up the machinery that eventually brought about the wars. It should be obvious that the way to win the world is to start with the individual opinion leaders, those strong, active individuals who have innate leadership capacity and want to be involved in the business of changing the world.

An adequate example closer to home concerns a popular heavy weight champion of the world. When asked by an airline passenger why he embraced a non-Christian religion his answer was clear. He said there was no way within the framework of Christianity to act in a creative way to change the world. He believed the church to be dead and lifeless. He found a group that showed him a way to express himself and gave him a plan of action for changing the world. He embraced it willingly and fully. This clever young man of talent and influence is only one of thousands who could have been won had the church been committed to Christian action; committed to changing the world.

The church not only lost the influence and leadership of the unreached; the church lost many of their ideas and ideals. What could have happened if the church had harnessed the energy and efforts of this generation for world evangelism? The people who are now burning the buildings of higher education could be stirring the fires of world evangelism. This same commitment, this same energy and involvement, could have been directed into the world ministries of the church. Somehow the church was too busy going through the motions of saving the world to be concerned about individuals.

Basic evangelism is reaching individual opinion leaders first. Then through the influence of such leaders, initiating an atmosphere conducive to multiple response and decision. A major growth factor of the urban church is that new converts have been a part of the city less than ten years. They are won before they lose touch with the common man. This has great implications for the church and the present urban crisis.

The new urban needs demand that the church treat the great metropolitan areas as city-states and understand the variety of groups and individuals present. The goal is not to reach the cities, ethnic groups, age groups or to build large conglomerate churches. The objective is simple to adequately minister to the needs of various groups so as to win individuals to Christ and plant New Testament churches within the city. Secondary goals will be reached automatically.

The gospel must reach every man where he lives and works. It is difficult to pull individuals out of their cultural context and expect to produce effective Christians. Each sub-culture can be won to Christ through a simple plan designed to reach individuals within their culture. A team of two or three converts from one group may be sent to evangelize a kindred group, but the success of the effort is in direct proportion to the identification of the "evangelists" with the culture of the people and their ability to communicate directly with the individual.

Christ selected common men as leaders because it was the common man who had gladly heard His message. Most of the Twelve were Galileans whose speech was distinctly common. Even a leader's wife who cannot adjust to a given sub-culture can hinder the progress of the Christian gospel. Church records show that a work among the American Indians of the West was significantly hindered because a minister's wife was afraid of Indians. It is clear that any soul winning team must program to reach individuals and train converts in the Christian faith so they in turn may lead their group to a saving knowledge of Christ. Only this procedure can assure the vitality and validity of the Christian message.

There is Biblical precedence for dealing with men in the context of existing social structures. The family structure of the Old Testament well illustrates God dealing with man within his social structure. The slavery and military domination of New Testament days are examples of the church reaching men within their social structure. Even Christ was known by His speech and His home town.

In Christ, most barriers are broken but language and custom remain a continuing problem. Individuals are uncomfortable outside their group and somehow the church has developed its own "Christian culture" that is often not compatible with God's plan for man. In fact, most of the theological differences within the church are in reality differences of cultural distinction and desire. This is why the simple "good news" delivered by an apostle of the street is usually more adequate than the "Sunday special" from the pulpit.

The static approach is inadequate for these days.[60] The church often goes from one extreme to the other. It is either busy extracting individuals from their culture in an effort to make them a part of a new society or it attempts to influence the whole group without first reaching the individuals who make up the leadership of the group. The church is to be the fountainhead for outreach evangelism but this outreach cannot be church-centered. An adequate concept of evangelism must be person-centered.

A theology that teaches the harvest of individual souls and has the sanction of Apostolic example must be concerned for the contemporary needs of individuals. It is the people that matter but more than this it is the individual who must be won. Out of every nation, kindred, tongue and people, God saves individuals who become Christian witnesses to their own. The goal of evangelism is not to build a corporate structure but to reach men with the gospel and house them in a New Testament fellowship that is truly Christian.

True expansion of the church is indigenous. This means that the church must program for individuals within the context of their group. The extremes of an individualistic society and pluralistic programming have hindered the progress of evangelism but recent trends are encouraging. The church must somehow see the overall culture and not lose sight of the individual and his personal needs. Individual conversions can materialize into simultaneous decision making by families, groups or whole cities, when the message of Christ is adequately presented. Groups are aggregates of individuals. So it is individuals that the church must reach. However, when a significant number of key individuals are reached, a whole group of people can often be truly influenced by the Christian message.

A people is more than a group of individuals. It is a social organism which by interaction within a structural framework confines activity to the social group. This social group normally considers itself to be a separate group and must be approached with this in mind. However, church growth takes place when individuals are reached.

This seems to be more obvious in foreign missions than in today's urban society. But if these principles are at work in world missions, it is obvious that they are at work in the church everywhere. Understanding how people act as a group and how the individual fits into his respective group can greatly enhance the potential advance of Christianity.

Faith, Fire and Fumigation

(Renewal-Centered Problems)

Somehow in the whole scheme of renewal, the dynamic structure of the church is disregarded and the automatic nature of revival is frustrated. A basic problem is the neglect of the priesthood of believers which causes a "passive sheep" structure to prevail within the church and generally leads to the church taking a wrong route to renewal. The courage to prune personnel and programs and to administer the cure for spiritual disease is almost nonexistent. Both clergy and laity seem to be preoccupied with program, personnel, organization or fellowship at the expense of renewal. Consequently, men unintentionally hinder the process of renewal in the life of the church.

29. Dynamic Structure Is Disregarded
30. Purpose of Revival Is Frustrated
31. Priesthood of Believers Is Neglected
32. A "Passive Sheep" Structure Prevails
33. Wrong Route Is Taken to Renewal
34. Courage to Prune Is Almost Nonexistent
35. Men Unintentionally Hinder

29.

Dynamic Structure
Is
Disregarded

Somehow in the standard growth scheme churchmen
disregard the dynamic structure of the church and frus-
trate the automatic nature of renewal. The phenomenon
of church growth is complex, but when the church grows,
a definite plan is discernible.

The developmental process creates both a formal and
an informal structure. This structure is modified pro-
gressively by processes operating within the church as
it evolves into an institution. If the church survives, formal
rules are increasingly imposed upon members that are
no longer a product of primarily voluntary interaction.
It seems that this rigid administration of growth tends
to increase efficiency for a time. Ultimately, however,
it produces a vicious cycle that impairs the effectiveness
of the church. The church may then collapse unless there
is a relaxation of the formal regulations and an increased
stress upon informal relations or the emergence of dynamic new leadership.

In time, with cultural and economic advance, sociologists say, churches attain a level of denominational re-
spectability: Their numbers increase and their church

170

property becomes aesthetic. What is the price of this progress? Will it be a doctrinal compromise, loss of spiritual vitality, or an overemphasis on organization and education? Can a dynamic be discovered that can preserve and perpetuate the basic theology of the New Testament and permit relevant communication through contemporary programming?

There are at least five anticipated stages in the development of a church: (1) weak association, (2) formal organization, (3) maximum efficiency, (4) institutional stage, and (5) disintegration.[61] These steps seem to suggest an ultimate disintegration or demoralization. However, if at the crisis point (A) which comes early in the institutional stage, creative initiative is brought to bear on the problem and the essentials of growth are properly supplied, growth should continue until the growth curve (A-B) is repeated. (See Figure 2.) The essentials of growth are: sufficient nutrients, energy in usable form, time, space and the vitality of individual organisms. The spiritual health of the individual within the group is the key here.

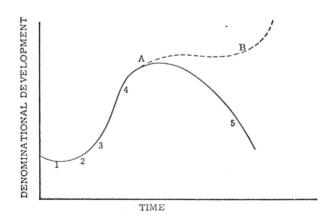

Figure 2. Diagram of five stages in the development of a church.

The stages of the life cycle overlap. No church remains the same as it passes through the cycle. The developmental stages may vary in length but probably not in sequence. Reaction usually sets in during the third or fourth stage and then renewal or death occurs. One thing should be clear: the stages are inevitable. The process grows out of a natural pattern of cause and effect relationship and under increased rational control, the result may be a constant adaptation of the structure rather than progression toward disintegration with its pathological effects. It is obvious that continuous adjusting and adapting to the conditions of environment is necessary for a church to remain in a stage of vitality. There are variables in the process related to longevity, but the most essential requirement seems to be a constant emphasis on the role of the individual in an effort to mobilize the entire constituency for continuous evangelistic action.[62]

Some claim that a church must lose the life and dynamics that nurtured it through periods of privation and persecution. Others ask, "Can the tide of institutionalism be stemmed and experiential, person-centered, individual religious experience be preserved?" There are two answers to this question: (1) the answer of the "determinist" of sociology, and (2) the answer of the "purposive control" advocated.[63]

History indicates religious movements like Judaism, Early Christianity, Church of the Reformation, and many modern denominations began as vital, dynamic movements, but lapsed into cold, lifeless formalism as they matured into institutions. The "determinists" claim the pattern of this sociological phenomenon is inevitable and that the life cycle can always be predicted. This claim is rejected by all who accept the validity of New Testament Christianity.

Optimism about the future of New Testament Christianity is based in part on the principles of the "purposive control" advocates who believe that human beings can exercise control and to some extent shape and direct the movement of which they are a part. Research in social or people movements has greatly advanced in recent years and has made much new data available. In the past, movements passed through the critical phases of growth and development without the aid of knowledge available today. Could it be that God expects churchmen to know and use available knowledge to maintain the contemporary ministry of the historic church?

The "determinists" claim the pattern is unalterable for all social movements, but the church is more than a social or people movement. The church is a divine institution with Christ as the Head. It is only the human element, and man's organizational structure, that changes and crumbles. The "determinists" philosophy is not applicable to the experiential aspects of New Testament Christianity. Also, a New Testament movement has strong eschatological implications. Christ will find faith on the earth! Christ will return for His Church.

Denominations are relatively new—scarcely four hundred years old—compared to the two thousand years since Pentecost. Lutherans probably are the oldest existing Protestant church, whereas Methodists are the youngest of the larger churches—less than two hundred years old. No one will question that these groups, as well as the younger churches, have drastically changed through the years. The concern is not for change *per se*, but for the altering of the scriptural position that affects spiritual vitality. It was not necessary to change theologically so that the needs of contemporary society could be met.

It is true that the very things that precipitate growth often are the causes of eventual decline in vitality. When the leadership establishes a bureaucracy and becomes more concerned with self-perpetuation than with maintaining doctrinal distinctives, the church structure becomes diseased. The institution becomes the master, not the servant, personalities are suppressed and its energies are directed into programs for survival rather than programs of outreach. There seems to be a preoccupation with the secondary.

With toleration from the outside and indifference on the inside, creeds of such churches become venerated relics and worship an empty formality. The institution develops a lack of concern for the individual and a pre-occupation with the needs of society as a whole. This loss of concern for the individual signals the complete internal collapse of the church as a religious force. Internal reform through spiritual renewal is the only means of restoring such a church to a position of usefulness and vitality. It is obvious that over-institutionalism eventuates disintegration of the whole because it neglects the vital role of the individual.

The church is not sent to save the world, the community, or the family; her mission is to bring the saving gospel to individuals. The Spirit of God deals with the world, the community, and the church usually in groups to prepare the way for the Word of God. The Word then speaks to individuals. Men are born one at a time and they must be "born again" one at a time. This suggests a dangerous misconception about "mass" evangelism. Actually, "mass" evangelism is a misnomer. What happens is "simultaneous soul winning," or "multi-individual" decisions.

Because the structure of a church is dynamic and the personnel and programming change, it is obvious that the church varies as it moves through a sociological cycle; nevertheless, it does not follow that the church must move through the cycle theologically. The experiential aspects of New Testament Christianity remain available to all believers of each generation.

So that corporate vitality can be maintained, the church must program for the individual in the context of community. Leadership ought to be watchful for signs for deterioration. Moberg claims the symptoms of disintegration are: "formalism, indifference, obsolescence, absolutism, red tape, patronage and corruption." Since institutions change more slowly than individuals, early awareness of these signs of deterioration is imperative. Purposive control must be exercised before the "gap" occurs between the institution and the constituency.

The historical record bears out two related conditions that strengthen and perpetuate the vitality of a church: the emergence of wise and creative leadership, and the demands of the times. Since charismatic leadership often combines with existing socio-economic conditions to initiate a religious movement, it is reasonable to assume that creative, God-anointed leadership could cope with contemporary conditions and breathe vitality into a church of which they are a part. Given wise and courageous leadership, any church should be able to shake off the binders and shackles of tradition, reorganize and redirect their energies to achieve progress and maintain corporate vitality.

Knowledge of the cycle should not make churchmen pessimistic nor cause them to falter in an effort toward progress. Christians are not building permanent structures or eternal institutions; the objective is to reach men for Christ in a changing world. Program and personnel may change; but the basic motivation and message remain unchanged. The purpose of the church is the same: to maintain Christian ideals, to edify believers, to reach the lost, and to be a Christian influence in the world.

Leadership must take advantage of the current sociological data so they may be equipped to exert "purposive control" directed by the Holy Spirit before the church advances to the point of crisis. The time is short for most churches. For others it may even be too late to renew the present structure. New and creative initiative by believers can bring about a new birth of freedom in the Spirit. This may mean the planting of a new church based on the principles of New Testament Christianity.

It is evident from the growth patterns that leadership must exercise "purposive control" and exert individual influence upon the agencies, departments, institutions, and organizations if the church is to grow. Without this individual purposive action based on an understanding of the church and the spiritual basis of its existence, there seems to be no way for a church to withstand the normal onslaughts of institutionalization and thereby delay, if not prevent, the disintegration that normally comes to most religious groups. The influence of individual leadership is the key.

30.

Purpose
Of Revival
Is Frustrated

Revival and survival are close kin. In the broadest sense revival means to wake up and live. The Old Testament root meaning "to live" readily conveyed the idea of "breathing in the breath of God." Revival seems to underscore the Source of this life in God. In the New Testament the Word seems to mean "to live again." The prodigal son who was dead became "alive again." Paul seemed to equate revival with "rekindling the dying fire" or to a plant which has put down fresh roots and "flourished again." The basic ideal of revival is the return of something to its true nature and purpose.[64]

The word for revival is used only seven times in New Testament Greek. Although the ideal is suggested in many other ways. The comparatively small use of the word was probably due to the New Testament covering only one generation and during this time the church for the most part enjoyed a remarkable degree of spiritual life.[65]

Nature seems to speak of refreshing and a renewal that comes from rest and recuperation. Revival is a refreshing that comes from the presence of the Lord necessary for the spurring of man to spiritual heights and essential to the vitalization of his spiritual life.

Life is an up-and-down proposition. Chart the history of man, the history of Israel, the history of a local church, or the life of an individual, and you will find mountain tops and valleys. The very law of life demands that there be a period of revival to quicken and to make alive in the individual and the church. The ongoing program of spiritual outreach makes this indispensable for the church. All who are not renewed periodically by rest and recuperation will soon age and die.

The basic laws of growth seem to demand stages that are not continuous. There is a recurrent element in growth. All growth is temporary and is for a specific purpose. Once that purpose is achieved there must be new growth. Nature seems to demand growing periods and phases for all of growth. There is an ebb and flow of the tide. There are seasons of waiting for growth to begin again. The law of life seems to demand periodic revival, restoration and renewal for continued growth and progress.

It seems that true growth of value can come only if care is taken to plant the seed properly and to nurture the tender plant to protect it from foreign elements that would rob it of its vitality. Without the farmer there would be no crops. Someone has to "bug" the potatoes, chop the cotton, thin the corn and pick the fruit. Revival requires the leadership of a husbandman, who is first partaker of the fruit, a man who understands the nature of the fruit bearing as well as the necessity for planting. This man must plant with a view of the harvest.

The success of the harvest depends not only on the soil, and the touch of the finger of God, it depends on the husbandman who cares for the growing plant. This seems to be an essential part of renewal. When the harvest does come, there may be many workers sent into the field to gather fruit. Adequacy in this respect usually points back to the leadership and nurturing of a faithful man of God. Revival comes with the sowing of good seed.

Some list two types of evangelism: mass and personal. There is really only one kind of evangelism. Mass evangelism is actually a misnomer. What really takes place is not mass evangelism but simultaneous soul winning, or multiindividual conversion. Two, ten or two thousand may accept Christ in the same place at the same time, but this is not mass evangelism; it is a group of individuals, personally and individually, making decisions for Christ. To see the mass effort as simultaneous decision-making helps to understand what actually takes place. All evangelism is personal in nature. The early church was born in a blaze of personal witnessing. Consistently, the early believers were busy in the marketplace, on the streets, in the houses, persuading men to believe and trust God as Savior and Lord.

Based on all Christ began to do and to teach, the New Testament Church continued through the enablement of the Holy Spirit and ministered to the needs of man. The Bible makes it clear that they were "daily in the temple and in every house," and that they did not cease to teach and preach Christ Jesus. This was not a structured program of evangelism; it was a spontaneous effort, resulting from individual dedication. Each house became an outreach for the New Testament Church. Each soul became a flaming evangelist. Each couple became a team in service for the Lord.

New Testament believers spent their time in basic evangelism. They were personally involved in the public ministry and individually involved in personal evangelism. Beginning at Acts 2, a period of about thirty years, personal soul winning was the unbroken operation of the New Testament Church. This was the most successful work. Through personal evangelism all Asia Minor heard the gospel in just two years. Personal soul winning was the effective arm of New Testament evangelism. It was the only thing that really worked.

New Testament concepts burned deeply in the hearts of such men as Wesley, Whitefield, Finney, Moody and others. As camp meetings, protracted meetings and brush arbor meetings became commonplace on the countryside, the term revival began to be used. Somehow the term revival and evangelism became synonymous. Herein lies the root of the present problem. The great evangelistic crusades, the revival campaigns, the church-centered and city-wide meetings were great and did much to stimulate the interest of the community and world in the church. But their purpose was misunderstood. Instead of revitalizing the church for individual soul winning and personal evangelism, the church seemed to sit back and expect the professional evangelist and the paid pastor to do the work of soul winning.

Somehow in the enthusiasm of the revival, the concept of personal evangelism was overlooked. Some seventy years ago Torrey and Spurgeon wrote the first books on the subject of personal evangelism. Since then, hundreds of books and articles have been distributed throughout the church in an effort to revitalize New Testament evangelism. But somehow, the church has not yet rediscovered this foundational truth. This is the basis of the problem.

All sorts of programs, ideas and themes are promoted to involve individuals in evangelism. Efforts to get individuals into the church seems to be the goal when the effort of the individual believer should be to get men to Christ. Converts will gladly come into God's house as a worshiper. Somehow church members become concerned about the corporate ministry of the church and fail to see the priesthood of all believers and the individual responsibility of each Christian. Each man joined with his brother was indeed the New Testament way. It was through individuals working together that the outreach was effective.

Somehow in the desperate effort of the church to build its constituency and survive the statistical report, many excellent programs and training classes were geared to get men into the church. But not enough has been done to prepare men to lead others into a saving knowledge of Christ where they are. No church building as such existed in the New Testament. Consequently, the sermons to sinners were not preached in a church house, but in the marketplace. The New Testament concept is to reach men where they are in the world, win them to Christ, and return them to the house of God as a worshiper. The church must stop evangelizing itself and begin to evangelize the world. Since masses of sinners do not darken the door of the church house, the gospel message must be taken to them where they are. A true revival leads to a rediscovery of basic New Testament evangelism and this evangelism is personal in nature. It demands a rediscovery of the spirit of New Testament Christianity and involves the individual in the work-a-day world as a living witness to Christ's saving grace.

The church building is no doubt vital to Christianity's survival in the twentieth century, but it is not a New Testament concept at all. It is probably the greatest single hindrance to world evangelism. Not because the church buildings hinder, but because it fences in the program of evangelism, and enables individual Christians to shirk from responsibility without being aware of the sin of omission. It places too much responsibility on the professional clergy and fails to advance the priesthood of all believers. This is not to say that the church building is not good: it helps in the winter and in the summer and on rainy Sundays. It also helps keep the people together so they may be trained and equipped for Christian service. This is its purpose and it must be kept in that perspective.

Evangelism is not to be centered in the church building. It is to be Christ-centered and is to be the center of the life of each believer of the church. The church is not a place to bring the sinner for conversion. The church is a place where Christians are trained and equipped to go out into the world where the sinners are and convince them to yield their lives to Christ and come into God's house so that it may be filled with worshipers and truly be a House of Prayer.

Revival in the church brings about a renewal of the spirit of man and awakens the community and makes it aware of the presence of God. The presence of transformed believers creates a sense of need and often causes men to openly confront the church. Evangelism, then, is the individual going forth into the community meeting each individual at his point of need and declaring to him the true story of Christ and salvation. Evangelism is designed to produce individual Christian action in the community so that the church may truly act responsibly.[66]

Either the church encounters this problem directly or it escapes to the sanctified island of the church sanctuary. The ministry of Christ was to identify Himself with sinners. He came to seek and to save the lost. Christ was concerned about the sinner. This was the purpose of His life, the reason for His death and the intent of His resurrection. The Holy Spirit was sent to empower believers as adequate witnesses in the world.

If men are to be truly Christian they must be concerned about sinners and identify with the sinner and his needs. To be truly Christ-like believers must take His message to the sinner: to the marketplace, to the street corners, to the mountain side, to the seashore and to the homes where the sinner lives. This may produce criticism, but it will also produce results.

This is the commission of the church. There is no escape, believers must meet Christ and then encounter the world or escape to the safety of the sanctuary and let the preacher attempt to do all the work. This is the great problem in the outreach ministry of the church and accounts for the lack of growth in most parts of the Christian Church. There can be no renewal without individual involvement.

31.

Priesthood
of Believers
Is Neglected

Major consideration in the program of evangelism must be the laity. To neglect the priesthood of all believers is to disregard one of the distinctive tenants of the Christian Church. This concept makes all believers as one in Christ. Each man may have a different work on earth, but each individual stands immediately before the throne of God as a priest and is under an obligation to minister. Each man is a priest to himself and to others. Christ is the only mediator; therefore, each man must feel an obligation for his own spiritual welfare and for the salvation and encouragement of others. Consequently, there is no difference between the clergy and laity in a spiritual state before God. The only difference is in the office they may hold. A basic orientation of the lay element is essential to add a significance to both the congregation and clergy. Each have distinct, Christian responsibilities but strange things have happened to this concept within the church.

A major dynamic of New Testament Christianity was the priesthood of believers. Every sincere worshiper had free access to the Lord Jesus Christ. Every Christian had a sacred calling and an obligation to serve in kingdom work. Consequently, the church was a fellowship of believers involved in Christian service. Literally, New Testament Christianity was a "royal priesthood" where all performed a ministry.

The concept was initiated deep in the Old Testament. God intended for Israel to become a "kinglom of priests" but somehow the idea did not materialize. Most likely this did not develop in Judaism for the same reasons the concept is being neglected today. As a rule, man's human nature does not enjoy sharing the role of leadership.

Judaism required the High Priest alone to enter the Holy Place once each year to offer sacrifice for the sins of the people. The Priest entered trembling and the people waited anxiously for his acceptance and return. As he walked back and forth ministering before the Lord, the bells upon his garments would ring. The people were aware that he was alive and performing his ministry but not until he emerged from behind the veil were they fully assured that God had accepted their Priest and had covered their sins. This annual event caused a complete dependence on the Priest.

The continuation of Judaism depended on the annual sacrifice in the Temple. Consequently, Hebrew ceremonialism produced a passive involvement of the people in the spiritual life of the nation. The Law was to be a schoolmaster to bring men to Christ, but when the time arrived, the people refused to accept Christ because of leadership. Therefore, God used Judaism's built-in destructive mechanisms to foster individual initiative. This was done in two stages: first, the veil in the Temple was parted to give each man access; secondly, the Temple itself was destroyed. With the complete destruction of the Temple the continued validity of Judaism was to be questioned if not destroyed.

The masses of the people were shut out of the presence of God and away from free access to the Mercy Seat by Judaism. The death, burial and resurrection of Jesus Christ opened this access and gave each man not only the privilege, but the responsibility of daily ministering before the Lord for himself and others. At the death of Christ, the veil in the Temple was torn in two and Christ entered into heaven making sacrifice of His own blood upon the eternal Mercy Seat for all mankind. Since that day, each man has had free and independent access to God but somehow the church still neglects the priesthood of believers.

Following the crucifixion, the leaders of Judaism immediately repaired the great veil in the Temple and continued as they were before in tradition, orders, ritual and ceremony separating the people from free access to the Mercy Seat. The Temple in Jerusalem was destroyed but many refused to follow the Christian way, preferring the comfort and apparent security of Judaism. Following the early spread of New Testament Christianity, the church began to build sanctuaries to "house the presence of God" instead of encouraging the Bible plan of each believer becoming the Temple of the Holy Spirit. A ministry order developed that separated the majority from their rights of priesthood. It was Martin Luther who rediscovered that the just should live by faith and not by ritual, ceremonialism or intermediate intercession. The free access of each individual to God was still valid. This brought about a resurgence of faith and a revival of religion.

When the flames of evangelistic fires began to grow dim, and churches began to mature into organized and structured bodies, history repeated itself. Protestantism could not shake the cathedral concept. Ministers could not resist the prestige of the pulpit. The congregation could not resist the comfort of the pew. Liturgy and ceremony prevailed. Christians became passive while the minister busied himself performing with great eloquence and pretended passion.

The New Testament made it very clear that because Christ was the true High Priest, each one who followed Him was also a priest and had daily access to the throne of grace for himself and others. Ritual and ceremony may have value but they cannot touch the innermost being of man. Only the compassion and intercession of a true priest of God can penetrate the carnal veneer and reach the spiritual needs of man. Only the sincerity and love flowing from the hearts of men in touch with God can strike a chord of response and bring spiritual melody and peace to the heart of man.

Not only does the church neglect the responsibilities of priesthood in the pulpit, the church disregards the reality that each Christian is and should be a priest under God. The Spirit of God does not dwell in a sanctuary built with the hands of man. God chooses as His sanctuary the hearts of men. Deep in the Old Testament, God laid the pattern for His holy priesthood. The ideal was to be fulfilled in the Christian Church. The church collectively was to be a priesthood and Christians individually were to be priests. There was to be no sacred days or seasons. No special sanctuaries were needed. God's Spirit would dwell in the hearts of men everywhere and they would carry the message of redemption to all men.

There is a division of labor. The church cannot fulfill its God-given purpose without a ministry, without governments and without teaching pastors. Gifted men are given to the church for such purposes but this does not necessitate neglecting to involve individuals as priests before God. To do so robs the church of total mobilization and prevents total evangelization.

The Jewish nation was a kingdom of priests yet there was an Aaronic priesthood to perform certain functions for the spiritual life of the nation. Likewise, the church collectively is a priesthood, yet there are chosen men who are to exercise the functions of special ministries and to assist in the equipping and maturing of the saints to do the work of ministering.

Christ alone is the High Priest and He alone can bring redemption to man. He is the true intercessor for man's redemption, yet through Him all believers have access to the Throne and because of Him all believers are priests in His church. There are indeed special ministries in the church but there is one general ministry to which all Christians are called. The priesthood of believers is valid today.

Every Christian as a priest is to offer sacrifices of obedience and praise unto God. The acceptance of this priestly service is assured through the intercession of the High Priest, Jesus Christ. Only when this priesthood of believers is applied to the whole church can the advance of Christianity be assured and the growth of the local church be effective. There is no other way for the church to be adequate for the needs of everyone.

32.

A
"Passive Sheep"
Structure Prevails

Most local congregations have developed an "active pastor-passive sheep" structure that complicates the whole work of evangelism. Converts believe they are saved to be served rather than to become servants of the Lord. This produces weak and dependent congregations that can do little to structure a program of outreach. Such a church has a "sheepfold mentality," where the sheep are curried and petted and the shepherd becomes a go-getter, do-it-yourself kind of person who leads his flock into green pastures and keeps them out of trouble. This prevailing concept of the local church must be transformed.

A spiritual congregation true to the Bible is a visible fellowship of people in a given locality who band themselves together because of mutual faith and trust in God. This band of believers is committed to sharing salvation with all men everywhere. The real potential of such a congregation where each member is a minister remains to be discovered. The New Testament gives precedence to the idea and a few contemporary congregations seem to be making it work, but by and large the church maintains a "passive sheep" structure. The church often disregards these words of Christ: "Behold, I send you forth as lambs among wolves" (Luke 10:3). Believers fail to venture into the world as witnesses.

A growing church has a missionary congregation and accepts the concept of total mobilization and active ministering for the whole group. It has a witnessing congregation. The entire group becomes a missionary society. Together all members form a special kind of community of holy and priestly people who belong to God and exist primarily for broadcasting the excellencies of His Name and His mighty works among men.

When this happens, the pastor becomes teacher, leader and fellow laborer in the vineyard. Everyone in the congregation becomes a minister. The gifts of preaching and teaching are used to create a new image of a ministering congregation. Smaller groups are involved in Bible Study, self-education and in person-to-person witnessing. As the Holy Spirit opens doors of opportunity and calls attention to the urgent need for harvest hands, the whole church gets involved.

The church has a responsibility to spiritually equip the individual believer for Christian service. Phillips translates the words of Paul in II Corinthians 10:15 to show the anticipation of development within the congregation: "Our hope is that your growing faith will mean the expansion of our sphere of action, so that before long we shall be preaching the gospel in districts beyond you, instead of being proud of work that has been done in someone else's province." Poorly equipped and unproductive saints are a tragedy in the church today. An underdeveloped congregation produces a nominality which is synonymous with "passive sheep."

A congregation of nominal members totally uninitiated into a New Testament ministry is the most regretable aspect of any church today. To change this picture would necessitate a drastic re-evangelization and renewal within a congregation itself and a fervent challenge to each individual to accept both opportunity and responsibility for serving in the kingdom work of the church.

Another fruitful activity for an adequate church is that of mothering converts and initiating new congregations. The many barren churches across the land is an indictment against both the clergy and laity. Those responsible for this "passive sheep" structure should be reminded that sheep that do not reproduce may become mutton. Disregarding this aspect of the problem, churchmen seem to be bent on building "dinosaur churches" that are too ponderous to be effective as ministering congregations. The size is not necessarily the problem. It is the passivity.

The difficulty seems to be that the larger a church becomes the more passive the congregation is in spiritual matters. Their activity is almost entirely social. The individual is lost in the crowd and in the process he loses his sense of obligation and responsibility. The "passive sheep" structure often causes whole flocks to stray and need to be brought back to the joy of obedience through hearing the gospel themselves. The "passive sheep" structure is brought about by stereotyped methods and threatens the future of the church by denying the renewal aspects of individual involvement.

As a church succumbs to a "passive sheep" structure the personal identity of members as active Christians is lost. The intended mission of the church in the world is perverted. The church is virtually paralyzed by a crippling organizational paralysis and an introversion. The whole congregation, the source of potent witness and ministry in the world, remains largely frozen and immobilized by fear and lack of faith.

The "dinosaur church" has built multimillion dollar buildings to be used only once a week. Even multipurpose buildings seem to have little purpose at all. The congregations are satisfied to assemble on a Sunday morning to hear a less than challenging address by a minister who has been too busy in secular things to prepare himself spiritually for his work. The congregation has become isolationists and seems to be ignoring the world while professing to be actively concerned about it. The concern expressed is social or political and has little to do with the spiritual needs of the human race.

When the masses are ignored and the church is ingrown, it is obvious that the congregation has lost its clear-cut sense of purpose. The church is caught in this organization dilemma and the congregation remains largely immobilized. The only answer seems to be a true revival and spiritual awakening within the congregation. This renewal comes through revived individuals.

It is obvious that what the church *is* determines what the church *does.* If the church is doing nothing, it must be because the church possesses nothing. The urgent need is for men to touch God on behalf of personal salvation and move the church to spiritual renewal and outreach ministries. The church is God's base for operation. Men are God's methods. Nothing short of a dedicated resurgence of the role of committed Christians will accomplish the needed renewal.

A major problem of the church is that it is only winning its own. This biological process is legitimate but illustrates a basic weakness in world evangelization. The Bible does teach "household salvation." It is the responsibility of each believer to win his own family to Christ. However, when evangelism stops with the family or when the church assumes that winning only its own is sufficient, an impossibility exists in the realm of world evangelism. For the church to grow, there must be a reaching out. The church must initiate a missionary stucture that reaches not only to the four corners of the earth but also to the street corners about the church building.[67]

Each and every member of the church must be equipped and inspired to carry the vital message of Christ to all whom they meet. Miraculous improvement in the growth and progress of the local church could be effective if this were true. Growth may not actually be visible to the local congregation. This is why it is so important not to place priority on numbers as the congregation moves about in a mobile society and as the church gives of its membership to plant new churches. When the church grows naturally it is because of a labor of love on the part of church constituency who give of their means and individual support to advance the Christian cause.

A church where the "passive sheep" structure exists has become a mutual admiration society rather than an advancing army. A lighthouse on the corner that shines only in the daylight can never penetrate the darkness of evil in the heart of man. Instead of a flaming sun that radiates the warmth of life, the church becomes a dead moon that still shines on by reflected light. The church has an appearance of life but is dead. With no life of its own, the church can give no life to others.

The time has come and God's church can become an adequate witness in the world today. It is not that the world needs successful churches, it needs adequate churches. Some would ask for effective churches, but this too has a taint of business norms and values. It is not whether a church is successful or effective. The question is, is the church adequate to perform the task incumbent upon it? Only when the question of adequacy is presented can one arrive at any understanding of what the church ought to be.

A church can achieve adequacy in size and spiritual ministry only when it has exhausted all of its possibilities of advancing. Any measure of adequacy must also consider the use of New Testament programming and the mobilization of the congregation for effective ministry. Passivity and indifference presently rob most congregations of an adequate witness.

There can be no justification for a retreat into cloister. Monasticism once before in the history of the church brought the organized body near to disaster. The church today cannot afford to fence itself in or to build walls between those to whom they are to minister. The fact that the world is becoming more wicked and even the fact that the world is encroaching on the territory of the church is not sufficient justification for withdrawal from contact with the world. Christian separation does not mean isolation or segregation.

The church must go into the world equipped with the Word of God and personal experience and meet men at their point of need with confidence that God's Word does work. Everything the church does should be motivated by mission and evaluated in the terms of its ministry to the lost.

God works. He has worked since the beginning. Christ continued the Father's work. Man is involved in the divine scheme to bring salvation to the lost. God continues to work through Spirit-filled men to renew the church and give it a continued thrust into the world.

God's continued working through the Body of Christ and in the lives of individuals is the present basis for the concept of growth within the church. The Spirit of God is in the shaking of the system that attempts to maintain the *status quo*. It is the Spirit that opens the door of opportunity, anoints workers and thrusts men into the needy harvest field. The growth of the church basically depends on the individual's willingness to be an instrument in the hand of God. Individual submissiveness to the will of God can eliminate the "passive sheep" structure and lead to continued spiritual renewal.

33.

Wrong Route
Is Taken
To Renewal

Most spiritual problems exist because the church is lethargic and indifferent to responsibility. Believers remain within the four walls of the church and let the community attempt to save itself without the help and assistance of the church. A few preachers march with those who dissent, but this is not the church in action. When evangelism meets people at the focal point of spiritual need, individuals are changed. This is Christian action. It is not community action or social action, it is Christian action.

Creative thinking normally takes place within a single brain and is then altered and tailored by the group. Therefore, it is logical to assume that creative spiritual renewal begins within the spiritual remnant and is then passed on in successive waves of acceptance to various elements of the church and society. Most churches seem to be taking a reverse look at renewal and revival.[68] The effort is often initiated in the minds of men whose spiritual credentials are inadequate to understand the experiential aspects of spiritual renewal.

Beginning with social action, which has a legal, political and social base, the church expects social action to produce better conditions for human progress. Believing that this will bring about sufficient change in the lives of people to create an awakening in the community and eventually bring about spiritual renewal within the church. New Testament Christians look at spiritual renewal from a different perspective: Revival within the church is the primary concern and the plact to start.

The secret of serving God and building a spiritual kingdom is individuals acting responsibly as Christians in their daily lives. This is where the real problem lies. The church is able to attract a congregation and lead them to participation in Sunday services as a group but has utterly failed in getting individual Christians back into the community to act personally as believers every day of the week. The problem is simple. A lack of individual Christian witness robs the church of simultaneous Christian action sufficient to influence the community for Christ.

The church has built congregations of spectators rather than individuals personally involved in worship. The church uses Sunday soldiers to fight the battle of the week rather than mobilizing the congregation for an all-out seven-day offensive. The corporate aspects of the liturgy, responsive reading or an occasional congregational hymn is not sufficient to equip or nurture individuals to become adequate instruments in the hand of God. Weekend warriors cannot win this battle. The church needs committed volunteers who are willing to wage daily war against the forces of evil in the world.

Renewal within the life of the church is a prerequisite to any spiritual development of the community. Evangelism is the indirect result of renewal. When people on the fringe of Christian influence accept Christ, it usually suggests that renewal is taking place within the church. But revival within the church itself deals with people who are already Christians. Revival literally means "to live again" and is produced by a new beginning of obedience to God. A new beginning of obedience for people who are part of the church initiates a renewal process that rejuvenates the spiritual life. It is a revival of the Spirit in the life of the individual and this normally takes place within the structured framework of the church.

Spiritual renewal within the church causes an awakening among uncommitted associates of the congregation and precipitates an awareness of spiritual need within the community. As the unconverted community grows in awareness of spiritual need, an awakening in the community normally points to the church as the answer to this growing need. This individual and collective concern often produces what is called "folk movements" such as the hippies or other groups of individuals who want to change themselves and change society but do not know how.

Birds of a feather flock together and society has various groups who demonstrate a growing concern for love, freedom, and other longings of the human spirit to be emancipated from the prison of human tradition. The soul music, the poetry, the literature, the revolt, the frustration of such groups, all point to their struggle for a new birth of freedom. These groups often awaken such desires in the lives of other members of society. They want to change themselves and the society about them but they cannot find a way. This is where evangelism begins. It starts at man's point of need.

A spiritual revival within the church brings about an evangelism based on penetrating biblical science. A theology of evangelism worthy of the name is intensely practical. Churchmen cannot domesticate God nor conquer His kingdom and make it an ecclesiastical colony. Basic evangelism and church growth can happen only when men cease their futile efforts to keep the kingdom under control and begin to let the kingdom control them. In trying to control and manage the commission, the church is robbed of validity and vitality. The Holy Spirit, through a conversion experience and spiritual renewal, directs the church to responsible Christian action in the world. This is evangelism.

Concerted Christian action by the church through individuals is New Testament evangelism. When individuals, because of the maturing and equipping ministry of the church, are able to act independently in their world as adequate witnesses, this is basic evangelism. A preacher in the pulpit may produce a worship response, enthusiasm or even repentance but his task is more than this. The minister's task as a preacher is basically indirect evangelism. He must prepare his people to become daily and consistent Christian witnesses. New Testament evangelism takes place where the sinners are. Evangelism is meeting man at his point of spiritual need. This usually cannot be done in the church building. Evangelism normally takes place out where the sinners are.

History has seen a successive parade of young rebels and changing fads and fashions. Each generation attempts to create a unique identity. Usually, their attitude and appearance, their music and literature, speak to the church concerning their innermost needs. Their music says, "We are open, we are listening, we want to know—somebody help us!" They speak of love and freedom and the church criticizes. Christians should be taking the message of Christ's love and freedom to this generation. After the Spirit has prepared the way and opened the door, the church must meet each generation at its point of need.

The steps to Christian action are simple. The church must decide whether to evade the issue and attempt to escape responsibility or to encounter the world at its point of need. Escape mechanisms are obvious. The church can continue to meet in nice buildings, sing nice songs, preach nice sermons, pray nice prayers, return to nice homes, work at nice jobs and drive nice cars, while the world goes to hell. The church can continue to explain their defeat by apostasy, last day evils and the "great falling away." These are simple excuses and will not hold up in the court of heaven.

The church must encounter the enemy on his own territory. The focus must be put on all of life. The issue is individual Christian action and this demands a decision for Christ and living right in the work-a-day world. This demands a life that is consistent with the Christian profession. This day demands honesty. Even a mongrel dog in the alley knows whether or not he is loved. An orphan, a dirty, helpless child, a hungry man instinctively knows whether or not he is loved. There is not way to camouflage this lack of concern. The church either loves God and man or neither.

Individuals must act responsibly in their world even though it is small. Any person who counts the number of his daily contacts can see the awesome responsibility for individual witness. There is no way to escape this responsibility. A person does not have to be rich or famous to have personal influence. Everyone has an influence on others, either good or bad. Christians must exert an adequate effort to influence associates for Christ.

The right route to spiritual renewal, then, is clear. It begins with renewal and revival within the church. This produces a new beginning of obedience to God on behalf of believers and precipitates an awareness of need among the unconverted and unchurched. This awakening outside the church opens the door of opportunity for New Testament evangelism. The church then must mobilize its full constituency to communicate the gospel to man at his point of need and through the dynamics of grace, transform and gather men into the fellowship of the church. In this way, individual Christians acting responsibly in the community can change men and the world. Consequently, the church will grow. Without individual Christian action, the church will surely grow weak, suffer from spiritual disease and eventually die.

34.

Courage to
Prune Is
Almost Nonexistent

When an individual attempts something new within the church, he is often immediately faced with an antagonistic confrontation with the keepers of the status quo. The encrusted structure of legalistic institutionalism is often so fixed that any attempt to renew the spiritual life of the church is met with real animosity. Change or new avenues of outreach seem to be an affront to leadership and an implication that God has by-passed their little system of operating the church. They cannot admit that church work is God's work. God's purpose for man does not change but God's approach to man has changed throughout the generations.

The church is considered as a human body and also as a growing garden. Perhaps men understand the nature of a growing garden better then they do the complicated mechanism of the human body. For that reason, the process of administering a cure for spiritual disease and the strangulated structures of the church can best be understood by looking at the horticultural practice of pruning.

In managing and administering church affairs, leadership must not only establish policies and programs, they must have the courage to superintend the execution of these plans. Leaders should be concerned with performance rather than policy. The task of leadership is to furnish a benefit and to manage the affairs in an effective and productive way. It is clear, therefore, that a wise leader would be watchful of disease and strangulation and would immediately consider ways and means of eliminating, not the symptoms, but the cause of the problem.

Occasional change is needed. Churchmen must have the courage to administer the cure for disease and strangulation within the church. Leadership must have full knowledge of the structure and function of the organization as well as a fundamental understanding of the theological practices involved before the process of pruning begins. Since the church is alive, it is obvious that care and due process must be considered before any aspect of the personnel or program is eliminated.

Pruning carries the connotation of fixing. There is a cutting-off aspect and a cutting back of certain parts for a better shape or more fruitful growth. Pruning also suggests the cutting down or reducing by eliminating superfluous and unproductive aspects. Pruning suggests the cutting away of unwanted material and in effect, a temporary reduction in the overall size of the operation.

In pruning away a diseased, broken or otherwise unproductive aspect of church programming, it should be fully understood that eliminating programs or cutting back on personnel, normally wounds the organism and initiates a setback. This "setback of pruning" is the basic phobia that causes churchmen to be unwilling to administer that necessary cure for disease and strangulation.

It should be remembered that the program of the church must be simple enough to be understood. As the program matures, it becomes complicated and difficult to explain or understand. It is these complicated areas that confuse the program of the church and hamper the mobilization of the congregation for effective service. These areas must be pruned.

Not only should there be a cutback of programs and a constant striving for simplicity and workability, there ought to be an evaluation of personnel. It seems that Christ Himself was constantly whittling down His congregation, confronting them with decisions that brought their true intentions to the surface and separated the sheep from the goats. In fact, on occasion, Christ actually insisted that His closest followers leave and return to their former labors if they could not find true salvation and consolation with Him. This precipitated the question and the affirmation, "To whom shall we go? Thou hast the words of eternal life." It is not quantity that necessarily concerns the growth of the church. The quality of personnel and programming actually brings about a climate conducive to growth and spiritual progress.

Planned obsolesence is not an entirely new idea. God initiated the basics of programmed obsolesence with the built-in renewal aspects of nature. The cycle of life, the reproductive process and the seed in the fruit all point to a planned replacement. The aged must be honored and experience ought to be respected, but new ideas and new blood must also be accepted as usable. It is evident then that personnel and program must change and give way to new and creative initiative. There must be courage to challenge the system, to attack the status quo and to prune unproductive personnel and programs.

In looking at the horticultural practice, it is obvious that pruning produces a wound. This is why much care and planning should go into the elimination of personnel and program. The objective is not to stunt the growth or to reduce numbers but to produce an effective and fruit bearing branch that will add to the quality and the quantity of the whole. It is not wise to lop off whole programs or personnel and leave stumps to remind people of the past or to leave monuments to unproductive programs. The pruning process should be done only with the objective of cutting back in such a way that new growth can flourish. The principles upon which the previous program was based should continue and the personnel worthy of involvement should remain effectively involved in some aspect of church ministry.

Pruning does not suggest an indiscriminant authoritarian approach to administration. A cut back in program or personnel must be done in such a way that the "set back of pruning" is kept to a minimum. As nature suggests, the pruning wound should be covered and cared for to prevent the entrance of extraneous matter that would cause decay. Pruning is not a process of just getting rid of dead wood or unproductive branches; the objective is seeking ways and means of causing more effective growth and more fruit.

There are times when old things must not be disturbed, but there are also times when the old and the unworkable ought to be discarded. There are times when leaders should remain in office and there are times when new blood should be brought into the growing body. It is this delicate balance that requires the touch of the Master's hand to make the churchmen adequate as administrators.

The whole purpose of the church must constantly be kept in mind. Good church administration requires the most effective technique available to be used to reach the ends sought. Emphasis must be placed on principle and people in contrast to policy and procedure. The goal is to move men to action rather than just precipitate decisions. The whole process of administration and all the procedures incombent upon church leaders should put action ahead of precision.

The organization of Christianity has always resisted regimentation. The principles of operation are the same but the practical outgrowth of these principles vary from culture to culture and group to group. The principles that suggest an adequate method of organization for action expresses itself in a number of ways. There must be a clear line of authority on the leadership level. Unity is necessary for executing and operating an adequate program. The general program of the church ought to be a number of small programs formulated according to general principles and operated as a unit. When any aspect of the program or any part of the personnel does not comply with the basic principles of operation, the situation must be remedied.

It is not necessary to remedy the situation with drastic changes but there usually needs to be a little pruning here and there to keep the overall picture within the framework of New Testament principles and practice. Leaders should strive to develop a program that is un-hampered by historic forms and structure the church for action and involvement. All the people should think of the church as a living organism rather than as a social institution with a multiplicity of activities. The purpose should be clear: the church exists for the nurture and equipping of saints so that saints may do the work of ministering and building up of the body.

The growth of a tree takes place in three places: (1) beneath the ground in the root supply system; (2) just under the bark in the support system; and (3) on the end of the branches in the fruit bearing system. All growth does not produce fruit. Some growth sustains life, other growth produces support, but growth in the fruit bearing region has a direct relationship to the perpetuation of life. All growth and development should concern the church, but churchmen must concentrate on the fruit bearing aspect to assure renewal and continuity.

Fruit bearing always takes place on new growth. It is this aspect of administration that should be the primary concern of churchmen. The fruit bearing apparatus must be kept in operation. New growth in the fruit bearing area also produces foliage. Foliage has a direct relationship to the food supply and the healing of wounds caused by pruning. In horticulture it is suggested that the pruning should take place as close to the main branch as possible so the growth tissue surrounding the wound may form new tissues to heal the wound. Since food moves down through the stems and comes from leaves above the wound, the wound must be in position near this food supply if healing is to occur. The implication here is one of distance. Pruning must be done close to the foliage and food moving mechanism if the plant is to survive.

Arbitrary and indiscriminate pruning at a distance from the main branch leaves a stump because the healing of the wound cannot occur. When church leaders prune or tamper with the fruit bearing mechanism of the church, it must be done with due caution and careful planning. The ultimate objective of repairing the wound and nurturing the whole body into a productive unit must be considered.

Where churchmen do not have the courage to prune, disease gnaws at the fruit bearing areas and the process of strangulation cuts off the flow of life to the superstructure. Without the courage to prune, it is only a matter of time until fruit bearing stops and the slow but sure process of death destroys the foliage, the superstructure and even the roots. The tree may stand but it is dead. There is no shade for the weary traveler and no fruit for the hungry. The structure is there, the organization is there, but the life is gone. This is the sad plight of many churches.

35.

Men
Unintentionally
Hinder

No man who claims Jesus as Savior and Lord would intentionally hinder God's scheme of redemption. Yet, because of the human element, men unintentionally hinder the spiritual work of the kingdom. The scripture is clear that the flesh has strong desires against the spiritual nature of man. There is a constant warfare: a struggle for supremacy. As tragic as this may be for the church, too often churchmen yield to the strong arm of the flesh.

Men hinder the work of God by wrong attitudes about Sunday. An easygoing, leisurely approach to "the first day" causes Christians to become indifferent about worship and witness all week. Many see Sunday as a replacement of the Sabbath: a time to rest and reminisce. Accepting Monday as the psychological beginning of the week they become materialistic and preoccupied with the daily problems of life. By failing to utilize the recuperative and renewal aspects of the first day, individual Christians grow weak and lose the vitality of the spiritual life. This greatly contributes to man's unintentional hindrance to the work of God in the world.

Tragic for the growth of the church is the subtle reversal of the commission which no longer reads, "as you go" but is interpreted to say "you must come." This failure to understand the commission has caused the development of a theology of coercion and forced the church to spend most of its energy attempting to challenge and motivate congregational involvement. No amount of human persuasion can adequately motivate a professing Christian to become spiritually involved in kingdom work; this is the work of the Spirit. Conversion is the internal motivation.

An artificial motivation may produce activity but not necessarily spiritual involvement. A multiplicity of methods causes churchmen to reverse the New Testament order: means, men, methods. Methods alone, even New Testament methods, cannot produce men adequately motivated to become the means to advance Christianity. Certainly men are God's methods but not just men; it is spiritually changed men who become the means by which the gospel is propagated. When the church permits manpower or methods to replace spiritual means (personal experience), they hinder church progress.

Overprogramming limits the mobilization of the congregation because complicated and conflicting methods confuse the constituency. Growth problems will persist as long as the church attempts to perpetuate complicated programs. The more difficult a program is to understand, the fewer persons will be motivated by it. Without total motivation there cannot be complete mobilization. When programs fail, often the personnel are blamed rather than an objective look being taken at the program itself. Consequently, the church perpetuates unworkable programs.

Obviously, the church has become imprisoned by the patterns of previous generations. In an effort to perpetuate the sameness of doctrine, the church attempts to perpetuate the same programs as well. When Christians have to be pushed or pulled into participation in the program of the church, something is wrong with both the program and the Christian. Involvement without results and motion without progress leads to emotional and spiritual exhaustion without worthwhile accomplishments. The life of the church becomes monotonous and boring. Everyone may be busy, but the prison of previous patterns forced upon each succeeding generation by their elders causes an adjustment to mediocrity.

An endless routine of activities which have little meaning overwhelm the people by demanding their time and presence until there is nothing left for the spiritual life. The tragedy of such busyness is that much energy and talent goes to waste that could be channeled by the Holy Spirit into real New Testament ministry. The church which keeps its people on the go day and night has confused the priorities of the commission. The going was to be automatic, the program was to be the making of disciples, but many ministers by walking the treadmill of churchly busyness produce feelings of insecurity and place undue pressures on the people. Until the clergy can get off the treadmill, the congregation cannot be led into meaningful worship and practical involvement in the work of the kingdom.

Too long the ministry of evangelism has been limited within the building complex and the present church constituency making the building the field in which to work rather than a force with which to work. The church does not exist to be a hospital for saints or a social club for sinners; its very existence indicates God's purpose: to evangelize the world. The church has become more interested in conserving things already attained than pressing forth to change the world. Churchmen perhaps fear that in changing the world, they themselves will be changed.

When conventions, seminars and workshops replace personal evangelism, decay and deterioration has begun. When the splitting of theological hairs overshadows the personal experience of believers, the Christian mission to all the world is in jeopardy. When believers lose the hope of eternal life and the imminent return of Jesus Christ for His people, the church sleeps, becomes lethargic and neglects the awesome responsibility of reaching out for the lost.

Only when the preacher himself can go into the streets of the city and be a personal witness for Christ can he adequately lead the congregation into evangelism. Regretfully, many ministers are busy with professional duties—arranging programs to get others to attempt to do what they do not have the inspiration or the spiritual "go ye" to do. For the most part the clergy has failed as "apostles of the street."

A basic human desire is to remain young and active. No one wants to get old until he does and then he wants to get as old as he can. Even incapacity and sickness are usually preferred to death. As long as there is a spark of life and consciousness, man wants to live. A similar attitude exists concerning many aspects of the church. A church is going to age, mature and become bound by tradition. No one is going to let the old ways die. Consequently, the tradition continues. The machinery is kept in motion even though the church is making no progress. Yet, many clergymen and congregants are unaware that the church is dying. This lack of awareness contributes to the mortality rate of local congregations.

Ministers often permit the downgrading of proclamation even though the people are still anxious to hear the Word of God. A minister is derelict in his responsibility unless he comes to the pulpit and speaks with one purpose: to bring about an encounter between the people and the Word of God. Instead of recounting and proclaiming the mighty acts of God, the preacher often makes himself the center of attraction and hinders the true nature of authentic preaching. The preacher is never sufficient within himself. No matter how thorough his exegesis, he must rely upon the Holy Spirit. Prayer is usually the most difficult part of his preparation. Notwithstanding, many men enter the pulpit plagued by the multiplicity of menial tasks performed throughout the week and are unprepared to proclaim the gospel. Unwittingly, they cooperate with the forces of evil that would hinder the progress of the church.

The major purpose of the church is thwarted when

personnel becomes preoccupied with the ongoing details of program. As conflicting purposes develop, the institution, which passes as the church, becomes something less than a church.

As various leaders begin to promote a multiplicity of personally related caused, the will of the people to follow is replaced by subdued antagonism. Personal incentives are lost. Inertia, discontent and conflict develop. The ensuing tension is a strong factor in the failure to maintain the purpose-centeredness of many churches.

When the vividness necessary to motivate involvement is missing, the gap between the pulpit and the pew grows. Neglect in the work of equipping the saints and lip service to the priesthood of believers widens the gap and brings about an indifferent participation in church programming. With some regularity the congregation simply gathers, gawks and grudgingly gives of time and means until many professed Christians suffer from spiritual sleep. The minister, too, is so actively involved in his work until he overlooks the potential and the problems of the congregation.

A link of understanding which connects the pulpit and the pew is weakened by these conflicting purposes and the chain of evangelism is endangered. The truth of the gospel remains within the four walls of the sanctuary or concealed neatly in the minds of the congregants. This isolation of truth segregates spiritual concern to the pulpit and deprives the church of the vitality necessary for growth.

Converts who become weak links in the chain of evangelism because they fail to develop the capacity to love, are usually the result of the preaching of cheap grace. When men do not measure the cost of following Christ and depend on an easy believeism, Christianity is robbed of the deep personal commitment necessary to make converts into apostles of the streets. The difficulties caused by the preaching of cheap grace and the tolerating of weak converts, compounded many times over in many places, have vitiated the victory strategy initiated by

Christ through a basic conversion experience.

Orthodox views are not sufficient to guarantee continued growth and progress for the church. After years
of effort to perpetuate doctrinal principles, little practical
Christian living can be found on the streets. The doctrinal
truth implanted in the head has not filtered through to
the heart nor influenced the daily lives of church members. Actually, much of the teaching related to a doctrinal
position handicaps the spontaneous application of truth
to life. A stereotyped approach to doctrinal truth often
limits the application to life because a doctrinal frame
of reference is difficult to cultivate. Only when doctrine
proceeds through experience into the heart will the New
Testament dynamic work and the truth prevail.

Churchmen obstruct inherent growth factors by neglecting long-range planning and the enlistment of new
leadership. They are more concerned about self-perpetuation and longevity than the involvement of new and
creative talent. This failure breeds unnecessary competition and personal strife among the staff and frustrates the whole function of the organization.

Churchmen do not adequately understand the phases
of growth and the stages of the developmental process.
This failure blocks the thinking of leaders into fixed attitudes and handicaps the advance of the church. Some
even think that statistics alone can measure the vitality
of religious experience. By ignoring key factors, the
growth and development are confined to periodic personnel changes and the turnover of adherence.

Churchmen hinder the progress of God's work by
thrusting men into areas they do not understand to work
with people whose culture or sub-culture is vastly different
from their own. This exploratory attitude brings about
slow and small growth and develops a theology of failure
which organizes to consolidate rather than expand. Consequently, the church settles for mediocrity in program
and gradualism in progress.

The church must avoid the numbers racket where a
"no holds barred" policy prevails in attendance building,

but this does not mean that numbers can be disregarded. Churchmen go to the extremes on both sides of this problem. To count noses and nickels alone as a criterion for growth would certainly be fatal, but to disregard the individual souls represented by the growth of numbers would also cause the church to die. Any willingness to stop short of total penetration of society will rob the church of spiritual health and bring about spiritual disease and stagnation.

Many maladies plague the church chiefly because clergymen do not practice preventative medicine. Other diseases encroach on the spiritual health of the church because of lethargic and indifferent congregations. A failure to communicate the Word is the basic difficulty and can be better understood by dividing the problem: one half is the failure of the clergy to adequately minister, the other half is the problem of laymen who evade God and fail to hear the Word when it is preached. Consequently, most churches suffer from spiritual malnutrition: a famine of hearing the Word of God.

Modern man is developing a unique ability to tune God out of his conscious mind. They have ears to hear but they hear only the sound without hearing the sermon. This happens because the congregation has little sense of purpose. With no desire to hear the Word they cultivate no will to grow and do not cooperate with God's plan or the preacher's ministry in reaching men. Satisfied and indifferent, the next step is spiritual decay and a resisting of the Holy Spirit. Such churches suffer from spiritual disease that is a sickness unto death.

The church is plagued by leaders who fail to lead or are unable to offer the necessary spiritual fervor to cause the congregation to follow. There is a lack of stamina. Initial reverses and discouragement settle in quickly to paralyze leadership at the first sign of opposition. Instead of intelligent action the congregation ends up with random activity. When leaders fail to lead, the church becomes strangulated in the area of program because communication breaks down between the pulpit and the pew. Inadequate programming definitely constricts vital functions of the church and prevents individual initiative which robs the church of the spontaneous response necessary for advancement.

Churchmen hinder the progress of the church by the building complex and the social structure of the congregation. The church building shapes not only the size of the congregation but influences the program and the attitude of the people as well. Since churches definitely grow in proportion to the group they are structured to reach, great care in planning the building as well as the program must be taken by all concerned if the church is to be an adequate witness in the community.

Many local congregations and individual Christians are unable to identify parent church activity with global Christian objectives. A "come" structure and a "sheepfold" mentality robs the church of the "go" strategy. It is obvious then when the church fails in its world mission, it fails on the local level because of a lack of global concern and perspective. By over-emphasizing the foreign concern churchmen often enable the congregation to escape local responsibility. Going to the next man, to the next home, and into the next town must be an intricate part of outreach strategy or new churches will never be planted. When churchmen are too selective in evangelism, when men are rejected because of race, culture, language or economic standing, the global perspective of the church is lost and the whole concept of dynamic reproduction becomes invalid.

Ministers often hinder church expansion because of a selfish claim that the people are their sheep rather than God's salt. An unwillingness to share or encourage Christian men to become the seed members of new churches causes the local church to become an end in itself. By failing to see individual Christians as a means of planting new congregations, churchmen greatly handicap the world mission of the church. Too often church leaders fail to become competent in the science of mission and are unfamiliar with the personal aspects of church birth.

In an effort to keep the congregation happy, many clergymen concentrate on a narrow definition of fellowship and permit a "no harvest" theology to develop. Groups meet and talk with the usual consensus that "something must be done" but the personal conclusion "I must do something" is never reached. They limit activities to preparing people to someday accept Christ. The antiquated idea of working without commensurate growth is plaguing the church in many places.

Some congregations never outgrow the early family concept of the church. They develop a program philosophy that says "come to see us if you can, but if you don't come we'll manage without you." There is an indifferent resignation to the presence of unconverted people in the community. Without being conscious of the problem, many churchmen have developed an attitude toward the outside world close akin to a "send them away" philosophy. Fearful that new blood or fresh ideas from the outside world would spoil the little family group, the church develops an easy going conciliatory approach to evangelism and a theology of failure.

Many churches attempt to cover up a lack of progress by statistics or a materialistic veneer. Some clergymen become almost professional in their ability to create an image of progress. An active spiritual drift within the congregation is so camouflaged by activity and good reports that the majority of the constituency is unaware of the desperate circumstances of the church. The seed of this problem may have been inherited from the previous generation, but it seems to be perpetuated by the pulpit.

Often the messages are watered down to eliminate elements which might be offensive to an uncommitted congregation. Much of the preaching is secular and false in terms of New Testament validity. The pulpit constantly nags the people into "doing good" and attempts to motivate participation in the social improvement of the community. The whole key to holding the church together seems to be "fellowship." This has never been a sufficient cohesive force to bind a congregation together; only the Holy Spirit and the Word can perform this spiritual work.

Some churches are plagued by a special kind of paternalism which programs and regulates the church from the outside. Often in an effort to maintain corporate fellowship with a larger body, churchmen force local congregations into cooperative programming that presupposes the same needs and same resources everywhere, rather than gearing the program to local needs. Creative initiative and programming are stifled and the natural capacity of the congregation remains untapped. There is nothing wrong with cooperative programs or centralized authority; it is the generalization necessary to produce cooperative programming that often cripples the local congregation. If a church is to be more than a "mission station" everyone must be totally involved in programming and local problem solving. This is the only logical course for progress and growth.

Many churchmen hinder the progress of the church by an over-emphasis on separation from the world. A growing church must have living connections and the best source for these connections is for converts to continue friendly relationships with previous associates. Becoming a Christian does not mean that one must desert his friends; it only means that he must separate himself from their sins. Friendship evangelism is still the answer to an impersonal society, because family and friends are much more easily influenced for Christ by intimates whom they have known and appreciated.

At other times the church fails by not impressing upon converts their need for separating themselves from the sins of their friends. There must be a contrast between the witness and the sinner. This means to live a life that is above and beyond the life of men in sin. Only then can they accept the Christian life as a better way.

Often the church is hindered by concentrating on

secondary projects. Certainly the building of cathedrals and the establishing of Christian colleges, seminaries, hospitals, orphanages or asylums have their place along with other religious and philanthropic causes, but they do not demand the priority normally given to them by most Christians. Such projects take much time and money to say nothing of the leadership talent involved. These are good and worthy projects and need prayerful and considerate attention of Christians everywhere, but they are not the prime concern of the church. The reaching of those lost and the bringing of men to Christ must have priority if the church is to grow.

Churchmen often hinder the church by failing to program for the individual. Not understanding society as a whole and the role of the individual within his group, the church fails to express adequate concern for man's personal needs. Consequently, the individual becomes lost in the crowd and remains unreached by the church. By reaching out for everyone, the church often fails to really reach anyone. By failing to reach key leaders of a group, the church stifles the spontaneous spark of indigenous concern. An adequate church must minister to the individual and through key leaders reach the remainder of his group. Then, through Christian influence, the larger community and society can be brought to the Christian encounter. This is God's will. He wants His church to reach out, to win the lost, to grow.

Obviously the hindrance to growth is unintentional. No man who professes a basic knowledge of Christianity would intentionally interfere with the progress of God's work. Yet the human element, when it is not completely dedicated to God and guided by the Spirit, can certainly produce havoc and heartache within the Body of Christ.

The days of revival in the House of Prayer and the days of evangelism in the market place are not over. The Word of God clearly points to a great spiritual awakening in the last days. There is to be a mighty move of the Holy Spirit, when both the old and the young will be committed to Christ and their daily lives be directed by the Spirit. This day is upon us! Throughout the institutional church, the spark of revival is being fanned by the wind of the Spirit. The cry of youth who want to be involved can be heard. Many ministers seek a return to basic New Testament evangelism. Many are restless with a lack of progress in the church. Alert churchmen are sensing the times and the seasons and are moving with God. This new sensitivity to the ministry of the Spirit through believers assures spiritual progress and numerical growth for the church. The church will live!

This growing spiritual sensitivity throughout the church is making Christians more conscious of individual experience. This, in turn, is making believers more concerned about their personal witness and is producing more Christians in the streets. Coffee houses, city parks, apartment complexes, public space in downtown hotels and motor inns are being turned into meeting places for the church. Christian homes are being used as extension sanctuaries for families to regularly communicate the Christian witness to their community and to their friends. There is a new awareness of friendship evangelism. The church will live!

Unorthodox as it may be, unwilling as some are to accept the methods of the Spirit, it seems obvious that God is moving throughout the world. Great awakenings are reported in Indonesia, in Brazil, in Chile and in various parts of the United States. It seems that the Holy Spirit is filling every vessel and using every available man in a program of total mobilization that will produce indepth evangelism and a great expansion of the church. The church will live!

It is God's will that men should be saved. It is God's plan that His church should prosper. It is God's promise that the gates of hell shall not prevail against His church. It is our duty to be sensitive to the will and the work of the Holy Spirit; to be available instruments in the hand of God; to be apostles in the streets

and ministers in the market place. As men yield to
the move of the Spirit in this day, the church will
be revitalized, outreach ministries will be activated,
spiritual progress will be made: the church will live!

Footnotes

[1] The revelation of this truth significantly altered my thinking about basic evangelism, motivation, programming and mission. I am indebted to Dr. Robert E. Coleman for this striking Master Plan of Evangelism (Westwood, New Jersey: Fleming Revell, Co., 1963), p. 108; Roland G. Leavell, *Evangelism, Christ's Imperative Commission* (Nashville: Broadman, 1951; p. 3.

[2] See Melvin L. Hodges for an excellent analysis of men as God's methods. Melvin L. Hodges "Creating Climate For Church Growth," in *Church Growth and Christian Mission*, ed. Donald Anderson McGavran (New York: Harper and Row, 1965), pp. 27-39.

[3] *Ibid.*, p. 32.

[4] J. B. Phillips, *The Young Church in Action* (New York: MacMillan, 1955), p. VII.

[5] Roland Allen, *The Spontaneous Expansion of the Church* (Grand Rapids: Eerdmans, 1962), p. 143. It is difficult to determine the impact of Allen's compelling challenge on my ministry. His insight as to the causes which hinder spontaneous expansion are of particular concern to me. His works *Missionary Methods: St. Paul's and Ours?* (Eerdmans, 1962) and *The Ministry of the Spirit* (Eerdmans, 1960) increased my concern for the pristine power and simplicity of New Testament Christianity.

[6] I am indebted to Heinrich C. Scherz for sharing his ideas on "The Treadmill Syndrome."

[7] Donald Anderson McGavran, *How Churches Grow* (London: World Dominion, 1959), p. 58. McGavran is a leader in the field of Church Growth. His study in the strategy of missions, *The Bridges of God* (London, World Dominion, 1855) and his volume on missions theology, theory and practice, *Understanding Church Growth* (Eerdmans, 1970) are milestones on the road to Church growth. These classic volumes have made immense impact on my personal philosophy; consequently, I may inadvertently quote McGavran without acknowledgement.

[8] I am indebted to Medford H. Jones for this jewel and other basic ideas gleaned from lectures and personal conversation. Dr. Jones' influence on this work is gratefully acknowledged.

[9] J. Waskom Pickett, *The Dynamics of Church Growth* (New York: Abingdon, 1963), p. 79.

[10] Pickett, *op. cit.*, p. 81.

[11] See Peter Beyerhaus and Henry Lefener, *The Responsible Church and Foreign Missions* (Grand Rapids: Eerdmans, 1964), p. 110. Elton Trueblood, *The Company of the Committed* (New York: Harper & Row, 1961), p. 21.

[12] Harry R. Boer, *Pentecost and Missions* (Grand Rapids: Eerdmans, 1961), pp. 47, 161.

[13] Medford L. Jones in his basic strategy for growth expresses clearly the need for a "dynamic vacuum." An essential element in creating this "pull factor" is the elimination of any gap between the pulpit and the pew by adequately equipping the saints for service. Personal notes. (1969).

[14] See Alexander McLeish, *Objective and Method in Christian Expansion* (London: World Dominion, 1952), pp. 8, 11.

[15] Dietrich Bonhoeffer, *The Cost of Discipleship* (New York: MacMillan, 1967), pp. 45, 64.

[16] Georgia Governor Lester Maddox.

[17] See Hollis L. Green, *Dynamics of Christian Discipleship* (Cleveland, TN: Pathway, 1963), p. 49.

[18] *Ibid.*, pp. 55-60.

[19] See Elton Trueblood, *The Incendiary Fellowship* (New York: Harper & Row, 1967).

[20] Boer, *op. cit.*, pp. 47, 161.

[21] Green, *Dynamics of Christian Discipleship*, p. 64.

[22] Pickett, *op. cit.*, p. 11.

[23] *Ibid.*, pp. 12, 13.

[24] *Ibid.*, pp. 13-15.

[25] See Coleman, *The Master Plan of Evangelism*, Chapters 6, 7 for a discussion of "delegation" and "supervision."

[26] McGavran, *How Churches Grow*, p. 18.

[27] *Ibid.*

[28] *Ibid.*, p. 19.

[29] *Ibid.*, pp. 19, 20.

[30] Pickett, *op. cit.*, p. 27.

[31] McGavran, *How Churches Grow*, p. 16.

[32] *Ibid.*

[33] Medford L. Jones, "The First Annual Church Growth Colloquium" (Milligan College: Emmanuel School of Religion, 1969). Personal lecture notes. Jones declared positively that when the church does not grow it is either diseased or strangulated. He diagnosed current maladies as: 1) malnutrition; 2) inadequate sense of purpose; 3) lack of will to grow; and 4) resistance to the Holy Spirit.

[34] *Ibid.*

[35] *Ibid.*

[36] Jones, *op. cit.* He asserts that an embalance creating a stricture in the area of leadership, program, property or social structure will stop growth regardless of the doctrinal posiion or the external situation of the church.

[37] Donald A. McGavran, *Understanding Church Growth*, (Grand Rapids: Eerdmans, 1970), p. 198.

[38] *Ibid.*, p. 291.

[39] *Ibid.*, p. 289.

[40] Vergil Gerber, "Starting and Organizing Local Churches Overseas," (Evangelical Missions Quarterly, Fall, 1969), pp. 28-36.

[41] McGavran, *The Bridges of God*, p. 26.

[42] *Ibid.*, p. 28.

[43] *Ibid.*, p. 31.

[44] *Ibid.*, p. 34.

[45] Charles Kraft, "Biblical Necessity for Church Growth." A lecture delivered at E.F.M.A. seminar, La Mirada, California, 1970. Personal notes.

[46] McGavran, *How Churches Grow*, p. 2.

[47] Alan R. Tippett presents excellent research on quantitive, qualitative and organic growth patterns in "Church Growth or Else." (*World Vision* magazine, February 1966), pp. 27-29.

[48] McGavran, *How Churches Grow*, p. 16.

[49] *Ibid.*

[50] See Tippitt, *op. cit.*

[51] *Ibid.*

[52] McGavran, *Understanding Church Growth*, pp. 262, 263.

[53] See Hollis L. Green, *Dynamics of Christian Discipleship* (Cleveland, TN: Pathway, 1962).

[54] McGavran, *The Bridges of God*, pp. 23, 36.

[55] McGavran, *Understanding Church Growth*, p. 270.

[56] Alan R. Tippett, "Authropological Basis of Leadership." A lecture given at E.F.M.A. seminar, La Mirado, California, 1970. Personal notes.

[57] McGavran, *Understanding Church Growth*, p. 198.

[58] Donald A. McGavran, "Focused on Church Growth," a lecture given at E.F.M.A. seminar, La Mirada, California, 1970. Personal notes.

[59] McGavran, *Understanding Church Growth*, p. 201.

[60] Donald A. McGavran, "The People Movement Point of View," in J. W. Pickett, *Church Growth and Group Conversion* (Grand Rapids: Eerdmans, 1969), p. 2.

[61] See David O. Moberg, *The Church As a Social Institution* (Englewood Clifts, NJ: Prentice-Hall, 1962), pp. 118-125.

[62] For more detailed application of sociological research applied to a denomination see Hollis L. Green, *The Degree to Which the Church of God Remains Pentecostal in Experience*,

ThD. Dissertation, Luther Rice Seminary, 1968. Published on demand by University Microfilms, Ann Arbor, MI, 1968.

[63] See Findley B. Edge, *A Quest for Vitality in Religion* (Nashville: Broadman, 1963), pp. 10-74.

[64] Robert E. Coleman, *Dry Bones Can Live Again* (Old Tappan, NJ: Revell, 1969), pp. 11, 12. This is an excellent study manual on revival in the local church.

[65] *Ibid.*, p. 12.

[66] J. Edwin Orr, "Revival and Church Growth." A lecture given at E.F.M.A. seminar, La Mirada, California, 1970. Personal notes.

[67] An adaptation of the Evangelism-In-Depth concept as conceived by Dr. R. Kenneth Strachan is a workable way of mobilizing the constituency of the local church. For an excellent presentation of church growth guidelines for an Evangelism-In-Depth strategy see Malcolm R. Bradshaw, *Church Growth Through Evangelism-In-Depth* (S. Pasadena, CA., William Carey, Library, 1969.

[68] J. Edwin Orr, "The Laws of Revival." A lecture given at E.F.M.A. seminar, La Mirada, CA., 1970. Personal notes. Orr's research and· scholarship determines the proper order to be: revival, awakening, evangelism and then social action.